At Issue

Green Cities

Other Books in the At Issue Series:

At Issue

Green Cities

Ronald D. Lankford, Jr., Book Editor

GREENHAVEN PRESS
A part of Gale, Cengage Learning

GALE
CENGAGE Learning

Detroit • New York • San Francisco • New Haven, Conn • Waterville, Maine • London

Christine Nasso, *Publisher*
Elizabeth Des Chenes, *Managing Editor*

For more information, contact:
Greenhaven Press
27500 Drake Rd.
Farmington Hills, MI 48331-3535
Or you can visit our Internet site at www.gale.cengage.com

For product information and technology assistance, contact us at

Gale Customer Support, 1-800-877-4253
For permission to use material from this text or product, submit all requests online at www.cengage.com/permissions.

Further permissions questions can be e-mailed to permissionrequest@cengage.com.

Articles in Greenhaven Press anthologies are often edited for length to meet page requirements. In addition, original titles of these works are changed to clearly present the main thesis and to explicitly indicate the author's opinion. Every effort is made to ensure that Greenhaven Press accurately reflects the original intent of the authors. Every effort has been made to trace the owners of copyrighted material.

Cover image copyright Debra Hughes 2007. Used under license from Shutterstock.com.

LIBRARY OF CONGRESS CATALOGING-IN-PUBLICATION DATA

Green cities / Ronald D. Lankford, Jr., book editor.
  p. cm. -- (At issue)
  Includes bibliographical references and index.
  ISBN 978-0-7377-5151-2 (hbk.) -- ISBN 978-0-7377-5152-9 (pbk.)
  1. Urban ecology--Juvenile literature. 2. Sustainable urban development--Juvenile literature. 3. City planning--Environmental aspects--Juvenile literature.
  I. Lankford, Ronald D., 1962- II. Title. III. Series.
  HT241.G737 2011
  307.76--dc22
                                                                    2010037581

Printed in the United States of America
  1 2 3 4 5   15 14 13 12 11

ED011

Contents

Introduction

In recent years established cities around the world have been attempting to find green solutions to lower pollution and resolve environmental issues. These solutions include traditional strategies such as reducing the use of automobiles and emphasizing recycling, and innovative strategies such as the promotion of green roofs. New York City, for example, has redesigned its urban space to include lanes for bicycles; Portland, Oregon has offered incentives for residents to use solar panels on their homes. While these efforts have made urban centers greener, many cities continue to struggle with environmental solutions.

In their efforts to become green, older cities are handicapped in a number of ways. For example, most cities are designed for automobiles, the leading source of carbon pollution. A new city, however, could start from the beginning, incorporating green technology and innovations from the start. A new city could consider renewable power sources and eliminate forms of transportation that emit carbon. A new city could be designed around green principles, eliminating many of the environmental problems that continue to challenge older cities.

Masdar City

A new, green city, in fact, is exactly what has been planned and is in the process of being built in Masdar City in the United Arab Emirates (UAE). Located eleven miles from the city of Abu Dhabi, the massive urban project was initiated in 2006 with an estimated cost of $22 billion; while the construction would require approximately ten years to complete, designers planned for Masdar City to be inhabited by 2009. Masdar City would occupy 1,438 acres and house approximately 45,000 people, 1,500 businesses, and accommodate nearly 60,000 daily commuters. When finished, Masdar City would be completely green, emitting no carbon pollution.

The goals of the Masdar City project have been simply stated: to build a green city with renewable energy resources that emits zero pollution. To accomplish these goals, a number of designers and engineers have relied on both traditional and innovative technologies.

Masdar will rely on a variety of sources for energy, including wind power, a solar power plant, and a hydrogen power plant. On the outskirts of the city, a wind farm will generate up to 20 megawatts of power; the mud and stone walls of the city will be embedded with photovoltaic panels, capable of generating 130 megawatts of power. Eighty percent of the water within the city will be recycled, and human waste will be transformed into fertilizer. Even the construction of the city has focused on methods that prevent excessive waste of building materials. All of these processes will work together to create a self-contained, renewable energy system.

The Masdar City project has also been dedicated to using no oil or gas. Automobiles will be banned from the city and designers have fashioned shaded paths for pedestrian traffic. For longer commutes in the city, designers have constructed six-passenger vehicles that would operate like a subway system and be powered by solar energy. All of these innovations would ensure efficient transportation within Masdar City and zero carbon emissions.

Challenges and Criticism

There have been multiple challenges for the Masdar City project. The city is being built in a desert that experiences high heat and sweeping winds. The BBC noted, "The inhospitable terrain suggests that the only way to survive here is with the maximum of technological support, a bit like living on the moon."[1] The desert locale means that access to water is also limited. All of these conditions have created obstacles for the project.

Other critics have focused on the politics of a 100% green city in an oil-rich nation. Masdar City, these critics suggest, is simply a show place for a country that that burns excessive fossil fuels. According to the *Living Planet Report*, the UAE has the largest ecological footprint in the world, and with the exception of Masdar City, the government has done little to address these issues. These critics also note the irony of an oil-rich country creating a carbon free city: how green, after all, is a city built from the profits of fossil fuels? The $22 billion utilized in Masdar City, they argue, would have produced a better return if invested in the country's older cities.

Despite these challenges and criticisms, most observers have commented positively on the Masdar City project. If less than perfect, the effort nonetheless promises to produce new innovations in green city technology. Even as an experiment, the project may answer an important question: is it possible for a city to be 100% green?

The Future of Green Cites

Since the construction of Masdar City is an ongoing project, it is unclear at this time whether it represents a wave of the future for green cities. On a practical level, many localities would find a project this massive challenging. Traditionally, most cities have expanded around commercial needs, and the idea of initiating an expensive project without a defined commercial need may appear risky. But whether Masdar City is repeatable around the world may be beside the point. In the broader sense, Masdar City is representative of an ongoing effort to balance the environmental challenges experienced by cities around the world. While few cities will be able to be pre-designed, older cities can nonetheless learn from the challenges and innovations of the Masdar City project. As mayors, council members, and citizens look for new ways to balance the environmental impact of urban life, Masdar City may offer a new source for a broad array of possible solutions.

Notes

1. "United Arab Emirates Builds The World's First Zero Carbon City," *BBC*, March 28, 2010.

Green Cities: An Overview

Terry White

Terry White runs an environmental consultancy from his home in Maryborough, central Victoria.

The United Nations predicts that by the year 2025, 80 percent of the world's population will occupy cities. In the following viewpoint, the author contends that today's cities are not even close to being sustainable. White believes that the city and the surrounding countryside must conform to nature's pattern in order to become sustainable. The following article outlines numerous steps that the public can take in order to create sustainable, green cities.

According to the United Nations, 50 per cent of the world's people now live in cities; and by 2025 the percentage of city dwellers is likely to rise to 80 per cent.

The problem with this is that most of today's cities don't even come close to being sustainable; they survive only by importing food, water, energy, minerals and other resources from farms, forests, mines and catchments. They also produce enormous quantities of wastes that can pollute air, water and land within and outside their boundaries.

As cities expand, rural land, fertile soil and wildlife habitat is lost. As a result, more pollution is generated as food is delivered to cities from further and further away. In China, for instance, government officials are talking about building 600 new cities by 2010, an initiative that could result in a further 5 per cent loss of that country's cropland. . . .

Terry White, "Greening the City," *Arena Magazine*, August 2000. Reproduced by permission.

The natural world creates pure air, pure water and healthy soil; it modifies the local climate; it stores and uses solar energy; it produces its own food; it consumes its own waste; it creates a benign environment for humans and wildlife and it continually maintains itself.

Unfortunately, cities do just the opposite. Because the shape of the city dictates the shape of the surrounding countryside, neither can become sustainable unless both become sustainable. This means that city and country must equally conform to nature's pattern.

Nature's Design Rules

Most current design, says American architect Malcolm Wells, is destructive of nature's life-giving functions. Our greatest challenge is to build in such a way that human needs and nature's needs coincide.

There is now a vivid realisation that vegetation on roofs, vertical walls and ground level plazas can vastly improve urban air quality.

Germans no longer leave this matter up to chance. The German Federal Nature Conservation Law explicitly forbids any further loss of natural services. This means that when developers seek building approvals from planners, they must show how their building will retain or enhance the natural services provided by the undeveloped site. In this way, the economists so-called 'free goods' or 'externalities' like oxygen production, waste assimiliation, groundwater storage, biodiversity maintenance and so on, are given a formal value in the decision-making process. If onsite harm to natural functions and services can't be avoided, then these services must be restored somewhere else, so that there is no net loss. This law has been responsible for some remarkable design initiatives. . . .

Create Clean Air and Moderate the Local Weather

In Europe, there is now a vivid realisation that vegetation on roofs, vertical walls and ground level plazas can vastly improve urban air quality. Many cities in Germany, Switzerland and France now have a combination of penalties and incentives to ensure that inner city buildings have green roofs. Dachbegrunung, roof greening, is strongest in Germany. As a result of a scientific inquiry into ways to combat falling air quality, the city of Mannheim introduced its own by-laws in the 1980s that require all flat roofs in the central business district to be vegetated. Esslingen's by-laws go even further—all roofs, even up to fifteen degrees in slope, must be vegetated. In Switzerland, 70 per cent of flat-roofed inner city buildings must be green.

These initiatives have been made possible by a range of specially designed products: rubber membranes for waterproofing; insulation to protect plants from the effects of heat rising from below; protective layers so the waterproofing is not pierced; recycled plastic drainage layers shaped like egg cartons so that water is available to plant roots on sloping roof surfaces; and rockwool growing mediums which are engineered to hold just the right amount of air, nutrients and water for differing slopes and plant requirements.

Solar cells ... will demonstrate the commercial capacity of renewable energy technologies to meet the electrical energy needs of an entire urban residential development.

In North America, the City of Portland is researching the potential of green roofing to modify indoor and outdoor climate, and the city of Chicago is planning a major roof-greening demonstration with the US EPA. In Canada, the city of Ottawa has concluded that:

Green roofs provide solutions to many of the practical di-
lemmas municipalities currently face, including infrastructure repair costs, noise pollution, scarce amenity space, de-
clining air and water quality, excessive inner city heat and
even recurrent summer beach closings. (Beckman, Jones,
Liburdy and Peters, *Greening Our Cities*, 1997...)

Live Within the Solar Economy

It is now crucial that we abandon further use of fossil fuels
and promote all forms of renewable energy. As an example of
the urban possibilities, the Sydney Olympic Village of 500–600
homes will become the biggest residential solar photovoltaic
development in the world. Solar cells integrated into the roofs
of the houses, along with energy efficiency and passive design
features, will demonstrate the commercial capacity of renewable energy technologies to meet the electrical energy needs of
an entire urban residential development.

It is also crucial that we cluster essential city services
around village hubs and invest in energy efficient public transport so that the energy impacts of urban transport are reduced. Today's cars use only about 1 per cent of their fuel energy to move the driver. By using lightweight carbon fibre
composites for chassis construction, and hydrogen fuel cells as
the power unit, public transport buses could be 74 per cent
lighter and 100 times cleaner than at present. In the United
States, Zero Emission Vehicle regulations become law in 2003
and Daimler Chrysler has announced plans to produce 100,000
fuel cell cars by 2005.

Use and Re-Use Rain Where It Falls

In nature, rain is intercepted by plants, transpired through
leaves, filtered through soil, distributed by streams and returned to the earth as rain....

Because stormwater is neglected as a resource it becomes a liability, effectively moving highly pollutive toxins, sediments and litter from the city's hard surfaces into the nearest creeks, rivers and bays.

In a Melbourne City Council pilot study at Ross House in Flinders Lane in the centre of Melbourne, plans are underway to change the script. On this roof, the rain that falls on the sloping galvanised iron will be filtered through roof-top vegetation, stored in a roof-top rainwater tank and used to flush toilets on each of the five floors below. As toilet flushing accounts for up to 25 per cent of urban residential waters, widespread adoption of this one simple strategy in Melbourne could save on water-supply operating costs and reduce the need for the Watson Creek reservoir. In Berlin there is an interesting precedent. All nineteen multi-storey Daimler-Benz buildings on Europe's largest building site have gardens on their roofs, and capture water for use in toilet flushing and garden watering.

Complementary water-sensitive design strategies for managing urban water include porous street guttering that mimics nature by allowing stormwater run-off to be filtered as it soaks downward through sand and trickles into porous subterranean drains that provide continous moisture for street plantings. Vegetated waterways and artifical wetlands also filter water-borne sediments and pollutants so that only clean water ends up in urban creeks. Efficient appliances reduce mains water use and rainwater tanks provide water for drinking and garden supply. Taken together, these design solutions use rainfall productively and reduce our dependence on external supplies. . . .

Produce Your Own Food

Current food production arrangements are a one-way street. Nutrients and energy flow from country providers to city consumers. The left-over nutrients rarely return to the farm. This production pressure from cities will finally drain the country.

Urban food production can lower farm operating costs and consumer food prices.

Indeed, we are not far from that now. Present allocations to irrigators have left insufficient water in the Murry Darling Basin system to maintain aquatic life in many of the rivers, and a recent Commonwealth study estimates that by the middle of next century many of these same rivers will be unfit to drink, and too salty to irrigate key cash crops such as vines and citrus. Forty per cent of our food is grown in the Murray Darling Basin, and the CSIRO is now talking about the need to 're-invent agriculture' because of the damage caused by present practices.

These trends suggest that diminishing per capita access to land and water will soon force cities to feed themselves. Urban agriculturalists point out that this has many advantages. First, it could drastically reduce damage to rural food production systems and the unpriced damage to the air, soil and water that accompany them. Second, it could re-integrate urban families with nature. Third, it could reframe sewage and garbage as valuable sources of food production nutrients rather than costly and repulsive 'wastes'. Fourth, it could reduce fossil fuel use. And the list goes on Urban food production can lower farm operating costs and consumer food prices; reduce the need for transport; and maintain polycultures and biodiversity.

In Brisbane, a Mt Gravatt main street development feasibility study has shown that food production can be successfully carried out in the city using microfarming methods like hydroponics, aquaculture and vermiculture on city rooftops. Local business proprietors intend to establish a rooftop demonstration farm in the heart of the shopping centre to show how food wastes from local restaurants and food shops can be part of a cyclical process of nutrient recovery. The scraps will serve, as a food source for worms (vermiculture); the worms will provide a food source for fish (aquaculture); the nutrient-rich pond and worm effluents will stimulate plant growth (organic hydroponics); the rainwater will supplement requirements for fish ponds and vegetable watering; and the resultant roof-grown fish, herbs and salads will complete the cycle by supplying the restaurants and shops. . . .

Maintain All Life Forms

Nature's diversity has been built up over six billion years of painstaking trial and error. We can be fairly sure that the organisms that have survived this trial period are superbly adapted to a vast range of natural conditions. In the years to come we will need to constantly refer to these adaptations as our models of sustainable agriculture, sustainable cities and sustainable societies.

But here again the prospects are grim. Bird expert and chairman of Australia's National Biodiversity Council, Professor Harry Recher, expects that fewer than half of Australia's terrestrial birds will survive the next 100 years.

One of the causes of the loss of species, ecosystems and farmland is urban sprawl. In Sydney only a few per cent of the original forest remains, and about 400 of the 900 native plant species in western Sydney are endangered. Around Brisbane, only 600 ha of the original 6000 ha [hectares] of rainforest remain. Current trends suggest that unless deliberately checked, this encroachment on fringing bush, coast and farmland is likely to continue as our population grows from 18 million (1995) to 23 million in 2020.

Just as Germany encouraged urban design innovation through its environmental law, just as the State of California has influenced the international design of the automobile by introducing zero emission legislation, and just as China has increased its chances of providing a reasonable life for its citizens by introducing penalties and incentives to reduce population growth, there are strategic decisions to be made. . . .

Regardless of how much we might want greener cities and cleaner agriculture, they will not be delivered to our door all in one piece. We will have to find the parts and put them together for ourselves.

2

Cities Are More Sustainable than Suburbs

Edward Glaeser

Edward Glaeser is the Glimp professor of economics at Harvard and the director of the Taubman Center for State and Local Government.

While many environmentalists view cities as having a negative impact on nature, urban areas are in fact more ecologically sound than suburbs. In New York City, for example, an individual utilizes less space than a person does in a "clean" city such as Portland, Oregon. Furthermore, most New Yorkers do not drive to work, eliminating carbon dioxide pollution. Unlike suburbs and urban sprawl, cities can grow upward, using space more efficiently. Unfortunately, many environmentalists have attempted to prohibit city growth. Instead of helping the environment, however, this only leads to new development in other places. The growth of cities like New York offers the best solution for creating a green environmental policy.

The patron saint of American environmentalism, Henry David Thoreau, was no fan of cities. At Walden Pond he became so "suddenly sensible of the sweet and beneficent society in Nature" that "the fancied advantages of human neighborhood" became "insignificant." Thoreau's like-minded heirs, including the urbanist, Lewis Mumford, praised the "parklike setting" of suburbs and denigrated the urban "deterioration of the environment."

Millions of Americans proclaimed their love of nature by moving to leafy suburbs while denigrating New Yorkers for living in the most man-made of places. In the eyes of the pseudo-environmentalist suburbanites, anyone who didn't care enough about nature to flee Manhattan's great glazed brick towers seemed worthy of both pity and disdain.

Environmental benefits are one of the many good reasons that New York should grow.

The Ecological City

Now we know that the suburban environmentalists had it backwards. Manhattan, not suburbia, is the real friend of the environment. Those alleged nature lovers who live on multia-cre estates surrounded by trees and lawn consume vast amounts of space and energy. If the environmental footprint of the average suburban home is a size 15 hiking boot, the environmental footprint of a New York apartment is a stiletto-heeled Jimmy Choo [brand of handmade women's shoes]. Eight million New Yorkers use only 301 square miles, which comes to less than one-fortieth of an acre a person. Even supposedly green Portland, Ore., is using up more than six times as much land a person than New York.

New York's biggest environmental contribution lies in the fact that less than one-third of New Yorkers drive to work. Nationwide, more than seven out of eight commuters drive. More than one-third of all the public transportation commuters in America live in the five boroughs. The absence of cars leads Matthew Kahn, in his fascinating book, *Green Cities*, to estimate that New York has by a wide margin the least gas usage per capita of all American metropolitan areas. The Department of Energy data confirm that New York State's energy consumption is next to last in the country because of New York City.

Is there any reason beyond civic pride to care that New Yorkers are true friends of the environment? I think so. Environmental benefits are one of the many good reasons that New York should grow. When Manhattan builds up, instead of Las Vegas building out, we are saving gas and protecting land. Every new skyscraper in Manhattan is a strike against global warming. Every new residential high rise means a few less barrels of oil bought from less than friendly nations belonging to the Organization of the Petroleum Exporting Countries.

Good environmentalism requires a national perspective.

Given how valuable development in New York is for the environment, one might think that environmentalists would be fighting the preservationists on Madison Avenue to ensure that New York builds taller buildings. But the ground troops of the environmental movement haven't yet got themselves around to being pro-development, even in places, like New York, where development makes the most environmental sense. All of those years of opposing new development have made many activists reflexively anti-growth. Almost every act of neighborhood anti-development Nimbyism, or Not In My Back Yard, gets wrapped up in a mantle of environmentalism.

Good and Bad Development

The great problem with being reflexively anti-growth is that development in America is close to being a zero-sum game. New homes are going to be built to meet the needs of a growing population. If you stop development in some areas, you are ensuring more development elsewhere. A failure to develop New York means more homes on the exurban edges of America.

In the 1960s, an environmental anti-growth movement grew strong in California. This group proclaimed that it was saving the San Francisco Bay, and group members managed to shut off development in their region. Some bay counties have enacted 60-acre minimum lot sizes. The environmentalists did stop development in their own increasingly unaffordable back yards, but they did not stop development spreading to eastern California, Las Vegas, and Phoenix.

In many cases, development occurred in places that were less dense and that had less public transit than the older places that the environmentalists had protected. The environmental consequences of this kind of environmentalism are far clearer, since the net effect seems to redirect development to places where it would do more harm.

Good environmentalism requires a national perspective, not the narrow outlook of a single neighborhood trying to keep out builders. As a nation, we need to think clearly about where new housing causes the least environmental damage, and we need to make sure that our land-use policies help that happen. A local approach can do more harm than good because dense areas are rich in protesters who push new housing out to where there are fewer people to oppose it.

With this broader view, we see that [New York City] Mayor Bloomberg's vision of an even bigger New York City is a great environmental vision. We also see that those preservationists who have arrogated to themselves the power to stunt New York's growth are not only enemies of affordable housing but also abettors of the environmental damage done by urban sprawl.

3

Cities Are Not Sustainable Environments

William E. Rees

William E. Rees teaches at the University of British Columbia's School of Community and Regional Planning.

In the 21st century, cities will grow tremendously. While a number of environmentalists have defended cities as sustainable, they seldom ask what sustainability is. Sustainability can most accurately be measured by the amount of water and land needed to sustain a given community. While cities may take up less physical space than suburbs or towns, they nonetheless utilize resources—such as agriculture—from around the world. Likewise, a city's pollution has the potential to impact many other communities beyond its border. As a result, cities around the world leave a large ecological footprint.

London. Rome. Sydney. Tokyo. Even for people who have never visited them, the mere mention of the world's great cities leaves many of us itching to pull up roots and go there to experience what they have to offer. Even my hometown of Vancouver draws people from all over the world, and can justifiably bask in the glow of its on-going recognition as "the world's most liveable city."

But there is another side to cities and their gravitational pull, which is only too evident in the swelling slums and barrios of cities as far flung as Jakarta, Lagos and Rio de Janeiro.

William E. Rees, "How Sustainable Is City Living," *Briarpatch*, vol. 35, June–July 2006, pp. 10–13. Copyright © 2006 Briarpatch, Inc. Reproduced by permission.

The world is currently experiencing the greatest human migration in history—a worldwide rural-to-urban migration that has swelled the population of the world's cities by fifty percent, from two billion in 1985 to three billion in 2002, and which is expected to add another 2.2 billion people to the world's cities by 2030. This means that in just three decades the urban population alone is expected to grow by the equivalent of the total human population in the early 1930s. Think about it: cities will add more people in thirty years than the planet had accumulated in the previous 2.5 million years of hominid history. And most of this explosive growth will take place in the poorest of the world's cities, adding millions of people to their already overcrowded slums.

All of which raises a critical question: in an age of allegedly "sustainable development," just how sustainable are the world's cities, both rich and poor?

Defining Sustainability

To some analysts, this question is silly, even meaningless. They argue that people come to cities to take advantage of economic opportunities, to better themselves (ignoring the fact that many of the rural poor are actually being kicked off their land, victims of the land consolidation demanded by "structural adjustment"). These experts agree that the barrios are social disasters but argue that slums are temporary, a transitional phase that will be eliminated by economic growth. Just look at the seeming wealth creation that has lifted so many Chinese cities from the poverty mire in the past quarter century.

Appalled by pollution? No problem, say such analysts. Once people get rich enough to care about air and water quality, they'll deal with it. In the words of economist Wilfred Beckerman, "the surest way to improve your environment is to become rich."

Worried about resource shortages? No issue here either, now that technology can substitute for nature and thus de-couple the economy from the ecosphere. As Nobel laureate economist Robert Solow famously put it over thirty years ago, "If it is very easy to substitute other factors for natural re-sources, then ... the world can, in effect, get along without natural resources, so exhaustion is just an event, not a catas-trophe."

But is escaping our natural limits really that easy? Can economic growth and technological prowess really fill all the potential potholes on the road to global sustainability? If we look more closely at the biophysical and ethical dimensions of the problem, we will see that the answer is no.

First, what do we mean by sustainability? Analysts often avoid this question because of ongoing debate over the many conflicting interpretations. This is unhelpful because we do need criteria and standards against which to measure progress. On the simplest level, then, let me propose that something is sustainable if [it] can safely remain in its present state or maintain its present course indefinitely. Thus, a sustainable so-ciety might be one that is experiencing positive social, cultural and economic change—i.e., development—that does not de-grade the ecosystems upon which that society is dependent. Note that development, as defined here, can occur with or without growth in the economy. (Development means getting better; growth means merely getting bigger. The fact that we have confused the two for so long goes a long way toward ex-plaining the nature of the environmental and social problems we face.)

Ecological Footprint Analysis

But how can we determine whether a society is over-using its critical ecosystems? We can begin by applying ecological foot-print analysis, a quantitative tool I pioneered with my stu-dents at the University of British Columbia. The "ecological footprint" of a given population is the total area of terrestrial and aquatic ecosystems required, on an ongoing basis, to produce the resources that the population consumes, and to assimilate the wastes that the population produces, wherever on earth those ecosystems are located. Thus, a community that consumes large amounts of energy and material resources will have a substantially larger ecological footprint than an otherwise similar community that uses fewer resources.

The ecosystems that support wealthy city-dwellers' consumer lifestyles are often located in other countries half a world away.

How does the ecological footprint of our cities measure up? It turns out that the residents of the world's rich cities require the life support services of five to ten hectares (twelve to twenty-five acres) of global average productive ecosystem per capita, compared to the half hectare demanded by the poorest of the poor. By this measure, in 2001, greater Vancouver's 2.1 million residents had an aggregate ecological footprint of almost fourteen million hectares. This is forty-eight times the size of the Greater Vancouver Regional District, or about twenty times the area of the entire Lower Fraser Valley.

If this seems mind-bogglingly unsustainable, consider the world's largest metropolis. Tokyo's thirty-three million residents—about a quarter of the country's population—have a collective ecological footprint of 142 million hectares, or 1.6 times the equivalent productive capacity of their entire country! In short, Japan could not sustain even its capital city at current material standards if it had to rely solely on the output of its domestic ecosystems. These data show that Japan— along with most other wealthy consumer societies—has overshot its domestic carrying capacity and is running a massive "ecological deficit" with the rest of the world.

In effect, ecologic footprint analysis shows us that while modern urbanites may reside in cities, they do not actually live there in ecologically meaningful terms. The ecosystems that support wealthy city-dwellers' consumer lifestyles are often located in other countries half a world away. For example, most of the pollution generated by China's factory cities is attributable not to newly-urbanized Chinese, but rather to consumption by people living in high-income cities like London, New York and Vancouver. It seems that far from decoupling humanity from nature, technology serves largely to extend the scope and intensity with which humans exploit ecosystems everywhere—and globalization gives the rich access to just about everyone else's ecosystems.

The urbanizing human enterprise is destroying the habitat on which it depends.

Cities as Parasites

With every increment of economic growth, the human ecological footprint expands. So it is that modern high-income cities have become ravenous parasites on the global hinterland. And to complicate matters, the separation of production from consumption renders complacent urbanites both blind to the degradation resulting from their consumer lifestyles and unconscious of their increasing dependence on a deteriorating resource base.

This is no small problem because the entire planet is in a state of overshoot. The urbanizing human enterprise, losing touch with its ecological roots, is destroying the habitat on which it depends. The average human ecological footprint is 2.2 hectares, but there are only 1.8 hectares of truly productive land and water ecosystems remaining per person on Earth. To bring just the present world population up to average North American material standards, would require four additional Earth-like planets!

Ecological footprint analysis thus provides a biophysical standard measure for sustainability—our current "fair share" of 1.8 hectares per capita—and this in turn suggests an ethical directive for people concerned about sustainability: No lifestyle is sustainable if it could not safely be shared by all members of the human family. Vancouverites may be justifiably proud of the region's numerous innovative sustainability initiatives, but until we have made significant progress toward reducing our average ecological footprint from almost seven to a sustainable 1.8 hectares, this "most liveable" of cities will remain one of the least sustainable on Earth.

4

American Cities Can Be Green Cities

Theresa Sullivan Barger

Theresa Sullivan Barger is an author for and contributor to Saturday Evening Post.

While many people think of cities as non-green environments, Greensburg, Kansas, has proven that American cities are working hard to change that image. After a devastating tornado, the rural town of Greensburg was left destroyed. Instead of becoming another tale of disaster, Greensburg officials seized the opportunity to rebuild their town while meeting U.S. Green Building Council's Leadership in Energy and Environmental Design (LEED) standards, providing a message and model of hope for the future.

Sharon Schmidt, and her son Morgan were heading home to Greensburg, Kansas, when her other son Taylor called from an out-of-town high school trip.

"Mom, there's a tornado heading toward Greensburg. Don't go there," he urged, after watching a weather alert. But Sharon pressed on, into darkness, past downed telephone poles and power lines. They smelled gas from countless broken mains.

"The homes were all gone," she says. "Our big church was just gone. You could see from one side of town to the other."

"Mom, I think your house is gone," Morgan said.

Theresa Sullivan Barger, "The Town That Rebuilt Itself: After a Tornado Leveled Their Hometown, Citizens Vowed to Put Some 'Green' into Greensburg," *Saturday Evening Post*, May–June 2010. Reproduced by permission.

It was, along with about 95 percent of the homes and buildings in the rural town of 1,400 people. On May 4, 2007, a 2-mile-wide, EF5 tornado—the highest level—swept through Greensburg. Eleven people died, and nearly everyone lost their homes. Yet, in the wake of the destruction and disaster, city leaders saw an opportunity.

To attract people and jobs and induce young adults to return, they reasoned they had to be sustainable, reducing water and energy use and getting power from renewable sources such as wind or sun.

A Clean Slate for a Green City

"We had a clean slate, so why not do things right?" says former City Council President John Janssen. City officials envisioned a model for other communities.

Like rural towns across the country, Greensburg's population had been shrinking. Starting from scratch allowed them to design for the future. To attract people and jobs and induce young adults to return, they reasoned they had to be sustainable, reducing water and energy use and getting power from renewable sources such as wind or sun.

"We talked about smarter building, better planning, and better facilities," says city administrator Steve Hewitt.

Slowly, painfully, the town became more than another tale of disaster and death; it became a story of hope.

Unlikely Ambassadors

Before the tornado, most Greensburg residents had never heard of photovoltaic solar panels, tankless water heaters, and geothermal heating and cooling systems.

"We weren't tree-huggers by any stretch," Janssen says. "There was a lot of pressure to build the town back just the way it was." Instead, the city council voted unanimously to build municipal structures to meet the U.S. Green Building Council's Leadership in Energy and Environmental Design (LEED) platinum certification, the highest designation. To meet LEED standards, buildings are given points for each environmentally sustainable feature, such as using daylight rather than artificial light, installing water-saving systems, and using reclaimed materials like wood or bricks. The more points earned, the higher the rating. Both the up-front costs and long-term savings are usually greater with higher sustainability ratings.

Iowa-based John Deere Renewable Energy is building a wind farm.

"Everybody was pretty skeptical," says Stacy Barnes, 27, who works as the executive director of the 5.4.7 Arts Center and director of the town's historic tourist attraction, the Big Well, the world's largest hand-dug well. But today, about 80 percent of the community supports the decision to go green.

The Estes brothers rebuilt their BTI John Deere dealership facility to LEED platinum specifications, and Iowa-based John Deere Renewable Energy is building a wind farm to meet the city's power needs. In addition, the Dwane Shank Motors GM dealership that was rebuilt to green standards has become a corporate beacon. General Motors unveiled its electric Chevrolet Volt at the Greensburg dealership.

About 900 people now live in Greensburg, some from outside the area. The disaster got so much attention, including a reality show on Discovery Network's Planet Green, that cash donations, volunteers, and materials poured in.

"There's going to be a higher concentration of energy-efficient buildings in this small Kansas town than anywhere," says resident Farrell Allison. Nearly all the homes were circa 1950 or earlier, so most new homes are more energy efficient and contain more insulation and better windows.

Faith in the Future

Greensburg is a deeply religious community. When the tornado struck, "I know God's name was on everyone's lips. We don't have a basement. I believe God placed us where we were," says Schmidt. "The toll could have been hundreds of deaths." The fire chief ordered 300 body bags.

Losing everything changed priorities. "You learn that your family is more important than things," says Alexsis Fleener, 17, a high school senior. But people also saw this as an opportunity to "change the world," says Taylor Schmidt, who, like Alexsis, was a co-founder of the high school's green club.

"We're all part of the same environment. We all breathe the same air and drink the same water," says Daniel Wallach, executive director of GreenTown, a nonprofit organization created to help Greensburg rebuild sustainably. "We can agree that we are concerned about the future for our children."

The city's leaders are routinely asked to educate others about the greening of Greensburg.

Darin Headrick, the school superintendent, certainly felt that way. He promised school would open 88 days after the tornado struck. Classes met in temporary buildings at first, and nearly 75 percent of the students returned.

Headrick's commitment played a pivotal role in bringing people back. If children had to be educated in other towns, more families would have left permanently. The new school building will open this fall. The students themselves have helped with construction of the school, which will be a place of learning for kids and visitors alike.

"The mechanical stuff inside the building will have glass windows so you can see how everything works," Alexsis says. She wanted to be a veterinarian, but now plans to study sustainability and community planning in college. "The green movement changed me and what I wanted to do."

Hewitt and his staff still face struggles and conflicts. "The jury is still out on us," Hewitt says. "I think we've come an amazing way in two and a half years."

The city's leaders, such as Hewitt, are routinely asked to speak and educate others about the greening of Greensburg. "We're the new pioneers of the 21st century. In Greensburg, Kansas, everybody is doing what they can, at whatever level they can. We've all got to start making a difference."

People made a difference for Sharon Schmidt after she and her son Taylor lost their home. Volunteers from a Mennonite group built Schmidt's new home using energy-efficient, tornado-resistant Insulated Concrete Form (ICF) blocks.

"If you're going to come back in western Kansas, you've got to have something going for you," adds Schmidt. "I think it's going to be a model city 10 years down the road. I feel excited for Taylor's generation."

5

Green Cities Need Green Transportation

PR Newswire

PR Newswire is a leading global vendor in information and news distribution services for professional communicators.

In the following viewpoint, Gary Dirks—a renewable energy expert—maintains that transportation is the weakness in America's efforts to go green. Dirks argues that wind, solar, nuclear, and hydro energy all will have roles in the future, but that there's only one way to move transportation vehicles—oil. Nascent technologies and techniques that generate a fuel for cars from renewable materials are in the works and need to be continued.

In America's efforts to go green, our Achilles' heel is transportation; cars, trucks, and buses represent 29 percent of U.S. energy use, according to Gary Dirks, director of Light-Works at Arizona State University and a renewable energy expert.

Whenever U.S. officials talk about finding ways to end our reliance on oil, like now as a reaction to the massive Gulf of Mexico oil spill, we need to take a realistic look at how we use oil and what are our available alternatives, Dirks said.

For example, in our energy future "nuclear, solar, hydro and wind energy all will have growing roles in electricity generation, whereas the importance of coal and oil will decline," explained Dirks. "But when we want to move a car, a truck or an airplane, there's really only one way to do it—get the stuff out of the ground. Oil remains a relatively cheap source of energy that is so convenient its use overrides its considerable drawbacks in terms of air pollution, environmental concerns and national security."

So what can the U.S. do to end its messy addiction to oil but remain a mobile society?

'More research and development is needed to make these fuels a reality.'

Greening Transportation

"In addition to a long-term transportation energy plan that does not include fossil fuels, we need a nearer term solution that can take us from the traditional internal combustion vehicles to tomorrow's advanced fleet," said Dirks. "That future should include the Sun."

"There are techniques and nascent technologies in the works that will take carbon dioxide, water and sunlight and combine them in such a way to generate fuels for our cars, but today they are too expensive," Dirks said. "More research and development is needed to make these fuels a reality. That is why the U.S. Department of Energy (DOE) is sponsoring an energy innovation Hub to make 'drop in' fuels from sunlight."

"The beauty of these fuels is that they don't require production of any fossil fuel, which in itself requires energy and generates pollution, but are made from completely renewable, existing and abundant components—water, carbon dioxide and sunlight."

The process is similar to photosynthesis, by which concentrated solar energy is used in conjunction with carbon dioxide and water to create hydrocarbons. In addition to creating combustible fuels like methanol and ethanol, additional processing can yield more traditional fuels like gasoline, diesel and jet fuel.

Drilling will not be needed with these fuels. Increased security, cleaner air and new jobs will result.

"The fuels that result from these processes will look, feel and perform just like what we pump into our cars today. They will use existing refineries to prepare fuel blends and existing gas stations to deliver the fuel to today's cars," he added.

But the new fuels will be carbon neutral and will not add to the build up of greenhouses gases blanketing the planet. They also will help the U.S. move from an unstable source of energy produced far off shore, to a form of energy generated on our soil. Drilling will not be needed with these fuels. Increased security, cleaner air and new jobs will result.

The DOE Hub, along with several other ambitious initiatives involving both the near-term and long-term future of fuels, specifically looks at processes for making solar liquid fuels and bringing them to market in a developmentally rapid, 15-year time span.

"We need investments in the R&D phases of this technology to come not only from the government, but from industry too," Dirks explained. "And the new fuels will cost a lot more than the old fossil fuels they replace, at least initially.

"Even with subsidies, the cost difference could be dramatic," Dirks added. "Five dollars for a gallon of solar liquid fuel is a realistic short term target, but it could be more. So, we need to ask ourselves, do we want to continue with what is convenient and economical today or do we want to focus our efforts on what is the logical next step in our long-term energy future?"

6

Green City Transportation Has Drawbacks

Max Wideman

Max Wideman is a registered engineer specializing in project management consulting.

In many cities today, bicycling has been presented as a replacement for the use of cars. In reality, bicycles have a number of disadvantages in a city like Vancouver, British Columbia. First, unless one can afford to live in the more expensive downtown district, both bikes and public transportation offer a poor substitute to cars. Bikes also leave riders vulnerable in a crowded city and fail to protect them from many weather conditions. The bike may have many positive qualities, but it is not a realistic solution for everyone.

For some years now, the city fathers of Vancouver have been trying earnestly to improve the environment in our city. It seems they have been having some success because a recent front-page newspaper article announced:

> "Vancouver Home to Canada's Greenest Commuters—3% cycle to work, 17% walk.

More people in Vancouver walk to work than anywhere in North America except New York City. The proportion of people commuting by bicycle has doubled in 10 years. And the transit system, with triple the number of people using it to go to the University of BC [British Columbia] since 1997

Max Wideman, "Musings: Projects to Green Vancouver," *Max's Project Management Wisdom*, November 2006. Reproduced by permission.

thanks to U-Pass, has become so popular that it's in danger of losing passengers because of overcrowding."

Of course the press doesn't mention that there's been an increase in population of around 20% over the last ten years, but we'll let that pass.

I've been made to feel thoroughly guilty every time I step into my car to go downtown.

But the actual focus of the city fathers is on discouraging cars and reducing the number of car trips "to reduce pollution and create more livable cities." That presumes you can afford to live in close proximity to Vancouver's downtown area. Vancouver, like so many other cities is an expensive place to live in, and public transit is not necessarily the answer if it doesn't pass your door, or the schedule and frequency is not convenient. So, for those of us who find it too far to walk and don't have the puff power to cycle, it seems that the car is the only realistic option.

Still, I've been made to feel thoroughly guilty every time I step into my car to go downtown and it seemed only reasonable to fight back with my observations on the limitations of bicycles versus the merits of cars.

The Limitations of Bicycles

Bikes are bad because:

- Bicycles are highly unstable except when chained to a lamp post

- They will not stand up on their own

- Due to their inherent instability, the direction of the rider is highly unpredictable to anyone in the vicinity

- They do not protect the rider in any way, neither from unsafe conditions nor from the weather

- They are not a satisfactory means for most people to cover long distances

- Their capacity for carrying things is strictly limited, innovativeness of far eastern populations using three-wheelers or mini-trailers notwithstanding

- Six bicycles take up about as much room as a car for six

- Bike owners tend to occupy pedestrian sidewalks

- Except for tandems, they are individualistic and hence unfriendly, and tandems are only suitable for people who like snuggling close. Even then the potential is very limited.

- Modern bikes are capable of speeds lethal to the rider and are operated at these lethal speeds more frequently than cars

- Cable actuated caliper brakes are not a robust mechanism for speed control, and bicycle tires wear out quickly

- Anyone who has tried to cross the street at quitting time in an eastern city where bicycles are the norm will know that it is like trying to cross a twelve-lane highway—next to impossible

- Modern bikes tend to be worse than earlier models because they don't have mudguards and so make the back of the rider unconscionably mucky, to say nothing of anyone who happens to stand too close

- They require a lot of personal effort to operate, resulting in the operatives giving the impression of being superior and distant when they are really sweaty and uncomfortable.

We have to face up to the fact that we cannot survive without consuming.

The Virtues of Cars

Before extolling the virtues of cars, we first need to take a look at the proclivity of humans. Homo sapiens is an insatiable consumer. We consume from the moment of birth to the day of our death. We consume things like wool for warmth; wood for homes; and all manner of foods natural and artificial for sustenance often transported over vast distances; resources of all kinds for survival; to say nothing of a vast array of electronic toys to keep us amused; and space for all manner of activities like living, travel, recreation and growing things to eat. We have to face up to the fact that we cannot survive without consuming. For most people, what we consume is a matter of personal choice. We call that democratic freedom, something that we vigorously and rightly defend.

Within this context, it is understandable that people have a love affair with the automobile, because it has emancipated the individual more than any other mechanical invention. So, cars are good because:

- The car enables you to go wherever you want, at least on land

- You can go whenever you want

- You can go as far as you want

- It is safer than other means

- When not in use, it is no harm to anyone, nor is it consuming energy like public transportation. In these respects, it is better than the horse-and-buggy

- It is stable on its own

- It is less likely to be stolen, though in the city that might be a moot point

- It will carry a whole family together

- It can be used for carrying goods like the weekly shopping in one trip, or all the gear required for camping, fishing or the weekend ski trip and, yes, the kids to school

- Perhaps above all, it is a technological marvel within the reach of the individual, yet represents millions of hours of work (over the years) that has brought employment, wages, dignity and satisfaction to millions of people to enjoy what we now call our "standard of living" or "quality of life".

None of this is to deny the rightful position of the humble bicycle. It is simply to show that there is a group of people out there who are bent on promoting and launching projects designed to solve the wrong problem.

7

New Orleans Is Being Rebuilt as a Green City

Husna Haq

Husna Haq is a contributing writer to the Christian Science Monitor.

Following the devastation left behind by Hurricane Katrina in New Orleans, one particular need was new housing, and a number of architects pushed for a new vision in New Orleans: efficient and economical housing that created a greener city. One of the more ambitious projects was designed in the devastated Lower Ninth Ward with funds from the Bush-Clinton Katrina fund. Through the use of innovative techniques, architects are building houses, apartments, and community centers that are underpinned by green design philosophy. In the renovation effort New Orleans has begun to rebuild its future, offering an eco-friendly vision for the future of all cities.

When hurricane Katrina blew into New Orleans four years ago, Matt Petersen watched in shock as the floodwaters retreated, revealing one of the most devastating natural disasters in US history: billions of dollars in damages, 80 percent of the city flooded with filthy water, and a government response that provoked a firestorm of criticism.

"I watched everything play out in horror," says Mr. Petersen. "And, like everyone else, I went through the process of thinking, 'What can I do?'"

Petersen donated money and considered volunteering, but that wasn't enough. "I kept feeling this well up inside me, I felt compelled to act," he says.

As the city's cleanup began, Petersen, the president and CEO of Global Green, an environmental nonprofit that promotes green building, saw a silver—or green—lining in Katrina's catastrophic wake.

Four years after hurricane Katrina swept through New Orleans a bevy of green-minded government employees, nonprofit organizations, volunteers, and celebrities have helped transform the city into the frontier of a new green revolution.

"I began to think, 'Maybe I can do more.' I run an organization with big thinking behind it; it's a Red Cross for the environment. We have the greatest assemblage of green building expertise. How can we deploy that?" he says. "Certainly the city was going to be rebuilt. And this great city presented us with an opportunity to create the first truly green city in our nation."

A New Vision for New Orleans

So Petersen opened Global Green's first New Orleans office in March 2006.

Now, four years after hurricane Katrina swept through New Orleans, he and a bevy of green-minded government employees, nonprofit organizations, volunteers, and celebrities (such as Brad Pitt) have helped transform the city into the frontier of a new green revolution.

"Now more people are interested in what we do," says Wynecta Fisher, director of the Mayor's Office of Environmental Affairs. "That's what the storm did. I have had access to some of the best and brightest minds and techniques."

As a result, the city currently operates 49 biodiesel buses and several LED [light emitting diode] stoplights, with plans to purchase LED streetlamps soon. Green, energy-efficient schools are in the works, and the city is eager to do more.

"We serve as a model," says Charles Allen, chairman of the board of the Holy Cross Neighborhood Association in the Lower Ninth Ward. "This is how a community can recover from a major disaster. I say, look, we're going to prove to the world that you can live in an improved, better way."

As part of that "improved . . . way," Global Green came up with an ambitious three-pronged plan: rebuild 10,000 homes to be green, adopt a sustainable neighborhood model, and upgrade area schools to be more ecofriendly. Petersen also resolved to create local expertise in green building in order to create jobs and ensure that the effort endures.

In partnership with the city and using money from the Bush-Clinton Katrina fund, Global Green plans to improve energy efficiency and air quality of existing schools and open two new schools that will be certified Leadership in Energy and Environmental Design (LEED) silver. The schools will also help promote environmental awareness.

Rebuilding the Lower Ninth Ward

Global Green's landmark initiative is the Holy Cross project, a sustainable neighborhood in the Lower Ninth Ward that will serve as a model for other communities. To generate ideas for the project, Global Green sponsored an international design competition, challenging architects to design an energy-efficient and affordable neighborhood model.

The winning proposal, designed by architects Matt Berman and Andrew Kotchen of Workshop/apd, a New York design firm, consists of five single-family homes, an 18-unit apartment building, and a community canter that also serves as a sustainable design and environmental advocacy center.

The goal is for all construction to use zero net energy, and be carbon neutral and LEED platinum certified.

"The idea was to design replicable, affordable, sustainable housing," says Mr. Kotchen.

The homes, the first of which was completed in May 2008, are tall, narrow, two-story buildings wrapped in fiber cement siding and topped with photovoltaic-paneled shed roofs at 30-degree angles. Screened porches, lower roofs, and strategically placed energy-efficient windows accent the exterior.

Inside, the wood flooring has been salvaged from existing structures. Paperless drywall, or gypsum board, offers mold resistance in the humid city. Spray foam insulation prevents air leaks and increases energy efficiency. And paints use water- or soy-based solvents containing few air-polluting toxins.

Green design doesn't have to be expensive.

It's not just about the materials, though, says Kotchen. "It was the whole approach. For us, it's an all-encompassing design philosophy."

For example, he cites house and window orientation as ways to minimize sun exposure, and high ceilings and deep porches as natural cooling measures.

"Good design is green design," he says.

Responsible waste handling is also an important part of green building. About 8,000 pounds of waste are discarded during the construction of a typical 2,000-square-foot home, according to Sustainable Sources, a green building information resource. Global Green reuses or recycles construction waste to keep materials from being carted to landfills. This also saves disposal tipping fees.

Even the homes' landscaping is green. Porous pavement driveways allow rainwater to permeate the ground, rather than run off, carrying pollutants into nearby rivers and lakes. Rain gardens stocked with wetland vegetation border the driveways, ready to absorb and filter downpours. And shade trees planted in strategic areas—such as the sunny south side of a house—provide natural cooling.

This isn't necessarily new, but simply good sense, says Kotchen. "Good design has been around for a long time."

Affordable Housing

Contrary to popular thought, green design doesn't have to be expensive. The Holy Cross homes will sell for about $175,000 and are expected to save residents an estimated $1,200 to $2,400 each year in utility bills.

"There's an element of justice here," says Petersen. "The question is, how do we protect the environment and provide truly affordable housing?"

This is a theme throughout the Holy Cross project, including the 18-unit apartment building. The apartments, which will be reserved for low-income residents, are expected to rent for $550 to $650 a month.

Once complete, America's first entire LEED platinum certified neighborhood will include the first LEED platinum certified apartment building in the US.

"[The project] has created a ripple effect," Petersen says. "It's bringing in suppliers, creating a workforce. We're helping create a market. It's humbling, yet gratifying, to see what we've been able to accomplish to bring back this great city."

As reconstruction continues four years after Katrina crippled the city, perhaps the most notable rebuilding isn't happening at homes and schools, many people say. Instead, it's happening in town meetings and neighborhood associations.

"One thing that Katrina did, it made people really look at the importance of community," says Ms. Fisher of the Mayor's Office of Environmental Affairs. "People are engaged now. They're not waiting for the government to do something for them. They're getting involved."

In some ways, then, it could be called a perfect storm. "Absolutely, there are blessings and silver linings that come out of every disaster," says Mr. Allen of the Holy Cross Neighborhood Association.

The hurricane created an opportunity for New Orleans, he says. "We definitely have more friends, more resources at our disposal. It's allowing us to make major strides."

He pauses. "This is our chance."

8

The Green Rebuilding of New Orleans Has Drawbacks

Fred A. Bernstein

Fred A. Bernstein has degrees in architecture and law, and writes about both subjects.

Following the devastation of Hurricane Katrina in New Orleans, many people attempted to rebuild the city. One of the more noted efforts was a housing project in the Lower Ninth Ward, an area hit hard by the storm. A number of the new houses that have been built in the Lower Ninth have been named "Brad Pitt" houses because of the actor's involvement in the rebuilding effort. The houses have also become tourist attractions. Unfortunately, much of the architecture of the new houses is avant-garde, forsaking the history of New Orleans architecture. While the rebuilding effort in the Lower Ninth is notable as a humanitarian project, its impractical architecture has perhaps slowed the re-birth of the neighborhood.

Al Andrews who lives on Tennessee Street in the Lower Ninth Ward of New Orleans, said he didn't mind the tour buses coming through his neighborhood, but he wished the visitors "would give some of what they pay to the community." Mr. Andrews lives in one of the brightly colored, modernist houses rising on a small patch of the Lower Ninth, four years after it was devastated by Hurricane Katrina.

In 2007, frustrated by the slow pace of rebuilding in the Lower Ninth Brad Pitt set up a foundation called Make It

Right; the foundation then commissioned 13 architecture firms to design affordable, green houses. The organization plans to build 150 homes, all for returning Lower Ninth residents. So far, just 15 of them are occupied, but those 15 make a big impression.

New Orleans's Newest Tourist Attraction

Indeed, from the main route into the Lower Ninth, the Claiborne Avenue Bridge, it's impossible to miss the Brad Pitt Houses, as everyone here calls them. They are sprawling, angular buildings in bold hues not usually seen outside a gelateria [Italian ice cream shop]. Monuments to the city's resilience, and to Hollywood's big heart, they are also New Orleans's newest tourist attraction.

During my previous trip to the Lower Ninth four years ago, I mainly saw devastation.

Tour buses, including those of Cajun Encounters ... and Gray Line ... pass by the houses but don't stop to let passengers walk around. You can also take a taxi the five miles or so from the city's center to the Lower Ninth; the round-trip fare is under $30. (Virginia Miller, a spokeswoman for Make It Right, said the organization may eventually offer tours, but "right now the priority is getting residents settled.")

I drove a rental car, following MapQuest directions, to the intersection of Tennessee and North Galvez Streets, near the heart of the new enclave. I found that residents like Mr. Andrews and his neighbor, Gertrude LeBlanc, were happy to converse. "If we don't talk," Ms. LeBlanc, a cheerful septuagenarian, said, "how will people know what happened to us?"

During my previous trip to the Lower Ninth four years ago, I mainly saw devastation. Wrecked houses were everywhere. Now much of the debris has been cleared, and acre after acre has gone back to nature, with grass almost as high as the reconstructed levees. The main effect in much of the district is an eerie stillness.

The "Brad Pitt" Neighborhood

But "Brad Pitt's neighborhood" is a beehive of activity, with builders and landscapers vastly outnumbering residents. A sign in front of each of the houses gives the name and city of its architect. One, called the Float House, was designed by the Pritzker Prize-winner Thom Mayne of Los Angeles. The main part of the house is built to rise with surging flood waters, on pylons that keep it from coming loose. It's difficult to see the innovative foundation, but unusual external features are easy to spot, such as a kind of trellis cut into intricate patterns and painted turquoise, set against the raspberry-hued building.

The houses seem better suited to an exhibition of avant-garde architecture than to a neighborhood struggling to recover.

Nearby, an angular house by GRAFT, a multinational architecture firm, features a porch enclosure that looks as though it had been cracked open by a storm, an unfortunate visual resonance. A house by the Japanese architect Shigeru Ban has a private courtyard space between the living room and bedrooms, but none of the detailing that would make it feel like a part of New Orleans.

Indeed, the houses seem better suited to an exhibition of avant-garde architecture than to a neighborhood struggling to recover. A number of designers I talked to, some of whom had visited the neighborhood, lamented the absence of familiar forms that would have comforted returning residents.

Avant-Garde Architecture

James Dart, a Manhattan-based architect who was born and raised in New Orleans, described the houses as "alien, sometimes even insulting," adding, "the biggest problem is that they are not grounded in the history of New Orleans architecture." But, like other architects I spoke to, he expressed admiration for Mr. Pitt. "He deserves a great deal of credit," Mr. Dart said, adding that Mr. Pitt had "done more for New Orleans" than any government agency.

Jennifer Pearl, a broker who has several houses for sale in the Lower Ninth, has a practical view. "Brad has the very best intentions," she said. "However, had he come here with houses that looked like what had been here before, he probably could have had four times, five times as many houses up by now."

Another issue with the houses (except for Mr. Mayne's) is their elevation: to protect them from future floods, they have been built on stilts that turn their front porches into catwalks. The goal of porches is to create a sense of community, and that's hard to do when neighbors and passersby are literally overshadowed.

"It's like New York—you know, the skyscrapers," said Ms. LeBlanc, who lives in a single-story house next to one of the much larger Make It Right creations, like a Mini Cooper boxed in by SUVs. "And there are going to be more," she added.

A Slow Re-Birth

To most residents, the construction is simply good news. "It's hard living here now, but it's going to be worth it," said Melba Leggett-Barnes, a cafeteria worker, who is concerned about crime in the neighborhood. The lack of commercial activity is also disappointing. "We used to be able to go to the corner store," she said. "Now we don't have a grocery; we don't have a laundry."

Ms. Leggett-Barnes, whose house was designed by the Philadelphia firm KieranTimberlake, is—literally—the poster child for Make It Right; her image, plastered on bus-shelter signs around the city, urges former residents to return to the neighborhood.

"There may be people who want to move back," she said, "but don't know that it's possible."

Some visitors also make a stop at the other end of the Lower Ninth, on Andry Street, where three houses built by Global Green (another Brad Pitt-supported charity) stand bright and inviting—and unoccupied. The houses, by Andrew Kotchen and Matthew Berman of Workshop/APD in New York, are listed for $175,000. . . .

Unlike the Make It Right houses, which are reserved for returning residents of the Lower Ninth, the Global Greens are available to anyone. "We'd love it if you'd buy one," Ms. Pearl said, a hopeful lilt in her voice.

Local Agriculture Can Help Create Green Cities

Sophie Johnson

Sophie Johnson was an intern at The Nation *in 2007 and served as the editor in chief for the* Whitman College Pioneer.

In recent years, farmers' markets have become popular in some of the United States' biggest cities. Farmers have produced and marketed fresh agriculture products within urban environments, providing a healthy option within lower income neighborhoods. These markets have also helped revitalize communities within cities by providing a place for young people to contribute to community projects. Farmers' markets from Philadelphia to Boston have also made an effort to educate the public on nutrition and offer youth programs. Farmers' markets, like all agricultural markets, face challenges from agribusiness. But with farmers' markets growing, buying locally grown food can become an important step toward greener cities.

Marlene Wilx, a resident of the East New York neighborhood in Brooklyn, relaxed in the shade of her tent at the East New York Farmers Market and bit into a huge, bright-orange carrot on a recent sunny Saturday. "Would you believe I just pulled this from the ground an hour ago?" she asked, motioning to the half-acre community garden behind her. Wilx is one of fifteen to twenty community gardeners who set up shop on Schneck Avenue every week to sell locally produced fruits and vegetables. She's been doing it for nine years.

The East New York Farmers Market isn't just any old summer market; it's part of a multipronged, decade-old community venture called East New York Farms!, which endeavors to bring fresh, local, affordable food as well as sustainable living opportunities to the East Brooklyn neighborhood.

Local agriculture projects like East New York Farms! have become increasingly popular in the last few years as the effects of global warming grow more obvious. The fuel needed to transport foods across the country—or around the world—is a major contributor to America's enormous tally of carbon emissions, and buying locally means an automatically more energy-efficient way to eat. Farmers' markets and local food choices at grocery stores are popping up all over the place as a result: New York alone has upwards of 400 farmers' markets statewide this year [2007]—about fifty more than last year.

Revitalizing Community

Nationwide, groups are looking beyond the environmental benefits of local agriculture, and major social change is beginning to sprout from some local foods initiatives.

East New York Farms!, for example, was envisioned in 1995 by a group of local and citywide organizations who were brainstorming ideas for community growth in East New York—a neighborhood with a 31 percent poverty rate in 2000 (substantially higher than New York as a whole, at 19 percent). It had come to the group's attention that East New York was becoming increasingly starved of resources, lacking safe, meaningful youth programs as well as fresh produce and employment opportunities. The idea was to develop some of the vacant lots in the area into urban farms and to employ youth interns to cultivate the land. All this would culminate in a seasonal farmers' market that would provide space for community vendors to sell and purchase goods locally. In 1999—its opening year—the farmers' market brought in a few hundred patrons. Last summer there were almost 14,000.

And the internship program is thriving. Twenty teenagers—eight returning and twelve new interns every year—are selected from a pool of applicants, who are drawn to the program through high school guidance counselors and school presentations made by United Community Centers (the group that now runs East New York Farms!). This year fifty-four young people applied, according to Urban Agriculture coordinator Jonah Braverman.

"It's good for community members to experience intergenerational relationships," said Braverman of the internship program. "It helps youth and adults understand the resources that the others can provide." The interns, who work four days a week, including a Friday harvest, are responsible for everything from working in the garden to setting up tents and tables for the market on Saturday.

"I like it because it's one of the only ways to actually give back to the community," said Jason Thomas, 16, who is in his fourth year of working as an intern for the farm. His job involves training others how to plant, grow and harvest, and helping customers at the weekly market find what they're looking for.

East New York Farms! is not the only project using local foods as a means of salvation in low-income communities. Programs like it have picked up steam all over the country in hopes of building sustainable resources in communities that have until now been largely overlooked by some promoters of the local foods movement.

Local Food Programs

The Food Trust in Philadelphia is another successful example. The project, founded in 1992, has grown from modest beginnings: It now sponsors twenty-eight farmers' markets in the Philadelphia area, provides multiple nutrition programs to low-income schools, advocates for a farmers' market development bill at the Philadelphia General Assembly and works to improve access to supermarkets in underserved areas. Its mission is simply "to ensure that everyone has access to affordable nutritious food."

Although The Food Trust has been around for fifteen years, it has seen a lot of growth in the past few years, as awareness of the globalization of the food market in America has increased. David Adler, communications director for The Food Trust, sees this as only the beginning of a much bigger project. "Getting people to eat well . . . involves shaping the environment in a lot of ways: having an educated public, having the availability of healthy foods in communities, and having those foods be appealing to consumers," he said.

Local agriculture is making more and more sense as a means for social change—especially as demand for local produce increases.

The Food Trust has been especially successful with its unique public school initiatives: five separate programs that include everything from in-school, student-operated produce markets to extensive nutrition education courses at schools in low-income areas. There's even a *Healthy Times* newspaper that teaches students both journalism skills and health education, distributed by classroom teachers.

"It's important for kids to learn at an early age the importance of eating well," said Adler. "We work through training teachers to incorporate nutrition into regular lessons. It can be a part of every subject in school. We want to incorporate it into math, social studies, sciences—you name it."

The Food Project in Boston is similar to The Food Trust, focusing especially on youth programs that give teenagers, as its website puts it, "unusually responsible roles" growing, harvesting and distributing crops in the city. The Food Project grows almost a quarter-million pounds of food a year, half of which is donated to local shelters (the other half is sold to crop shares and farmers' markets).

The Seattle Youth Garden Works program was launched in 1995 to create opportunities and job training for homeless youth. As well as learning how to plant and harvest fruits and vegetables in one of two local gardens, youth are also taught how to write a résumé, track sales and inventory, and provide customer service, among other marketing skills. They also learn to cook meals made from garden-grown crops.

Local agriculture is making more and more sense as a means for social change—especially as demand for local produce increases. Although popularity of the local foods movement continues to swell, corporate agriculture remains a major threat to farmers. "A lot of the farmers that are small-scale are going out of business because there aren't enough people supporting them," said Braverman. "It's important to connect low-income neighborhoods and urban communities with people who are struggling to create a sustainable and just food system."

10

Urban Agriculture Is Not Practical or Efficient

Adam Stein

Adam Stein is a co-founder of TerraPass. *He writes on issues related to carbon emissions, climate change policy, and conservation.*

Vertical farms, or self-contained urban farms that operate within cities, have been promoted as part of the new green city. Unfortunately, the results fall short of the promise. The process of vertical farming requires a great deal of energy to maintain and the modern city is better equipped to house people than agriculture. Many people continue to believe in vertical farms nonetheless, judging that anything produced locally is automatically better. Farming, however, is much more efficient in rural areas. Green cities should concentrate on what they do best—finding spaces for people—and leave agriculture to rural areas.

Columbia Professor Dickson Despommier has generated a fair amount of attention with his concept for "vertical farms," stacked, self-contained urban biosystems that would—theoretically—supply fresh produce for city residents year round. *The New York Times* showcased outlandish artists' conceptions of what such farms might look like. Colbert did his shtick. Twelve pilot projects are supposedly under consideration, in locations as far-flung as China and Dubai.

The concept has captured the imagination of at least the sliver of the public (including the editors at *Worldchanging*),

Adam Stein, "Cities Are for People: The Limits of Localism," *Worldchanging*, August 8, 2008. Reproduced by permission of the author.

who laments the enormous resource demands of our food production system and yearns for something easier on the land, easier on our aquifers, and less demanding of fossil fuels. Vertical farms seem to promise all that.

Local is good, the thinking goes, and more local is better.

Is Local Better?

Promising, of course, is different than delivering. Construction requires a lot of energy. Keeping vegetables warm in winter requires a lot of energy. Recycling water requires a lot of energy. Generating artificial sunlight requires a lot of energy. In other words, the secret ingredient that makes vertical farms work (assuming they work at all) is boatloads of energy. No one seems to have actually done the math on the monetary and environmental costs of such a scheme, but they would no doubt be considerable.

Perhaps those costs pencil out (although they almost certainly do not), but the plausibility of the idea itself is in some ways beside the point. Whatever the merits of vertical farms, the enthusiasm with which this idea has been received suggests that we're becoming mightily reductive in the way that we think about sustainability. Local is good, the thinking goes, and more local is better.

Cities offer a lot of environmental benefits, at least compared to the alternatives. There are many reasons this is so, but they all spring from a fairly basic fact: cities are built for people. Lots of people, densely packed, sharing resources. Innovations that encourage or take advantage of that density are likely to make cities more sustainable. And innovations that undermine density have a lot of work to do to overcome their inherent environmental disadvantages.

New York City, for example, recently released an ambitious plan to slash municipal carbon emissions by almost two million metric tons per year. Fully 16% of total life cycle reductions will come from a new rail and barge network built for the express purpose of hauling garbage. No one will appear on *The Colbert Report* to plug the new garbage barges, but the system will eliminate five million vehicle miles per year. Less congestion, less noise, less air pollution, and less greenhouse gas emissions. New York's size and density make this project possible.

Efficiency is particularly important when it comes to housing humans.

Urban Homes vs. Urban Farms

Urban vertical farms, on the other hand, fail miserably on this score. Land is one of the primary inputs for agriculture, which is why we don't expect to see corn growing in lower Manhattan. Such spaces are better reserved for people, mass transit, mass entertainment, and businesses that depend primarily on human capital.

Our collective confusion on this point seems to be most acute when the topic is food. We intuitively understand that it doesn't really make sense to manufacture, say, iPods in small factories scattered across hundreds of urban centers, even though iPods are consumed in just about every city in the world. We readily grasp that the economics wouldn't work out, and we probably even understand that such a scheme wouldn't help the environment. Efficiency benefits more than just the bottom line.

Efficiency is particularly important when it comes to housing humans. Farming surely does stress the land, but so does suburban sprawl. Suburbs mean more lawns and more roads, for starters. Environmentally speaking, it makes more sense to move another person into a city than it does to make way for a berry patch.

iPods and food differ in important ways. But they don't differ as completely as some advocates seem to hope, and it really can make sense to house people in one place and grow food in another. Our food production system is, at present, undeniably in need of repair, but that doesn't mean that tomatoes in skyscrapers are the logical end point to which we should strive. (Note also that urban farms, community gardens, green roofs, etc. may have a lot of things going for them, but they don't exist on a continuum with industrial agriculture in the same way that vertical farms aspire to.)

As the world's population booms, we need to keep to continue growing and greening our cities. And that means keeping the focus where it belongs: on people.

11

Green Roofs Benefit Urban Environments

April Holladay

April Holladay is a science journalist for USATODAY.com, and lives in Albuquerque, New Mexico.

Green roofs are flat surfaces that work like traditional roofs but allow plants to grow in a layer of soil. While green roofs are more expensive than traditional roofs, they have the potential to last longer. Green roofs also have the benefit of creating lower roof temperatures, leading to an overall reduction of energy use. It is also possible that the growth of green roofs will help filter out pollutants that cause smog. Green roofs have been successful in countries like Germany and offer another way to expand ecologically sound policies in urban environments.

A green roof is a flat roof, usually, that has plants growing in a thin layer of soil, and works much the same as any roof. Its primary job is to shelter the building below from the elements: cold and heat, rain and snow. The plants and soil take the place of conventional roof coverings, such as built-up-roof (BUR), modified-bitumen or metal-standing-seam roofs. The plant/soil layer protects the roof waterproofing membrane, as do the more conventional coverings.

"Green roofs have the potential to doubling or tripling the life span of the membrane (compared with conventional covering)," says landscape architect Chris Counts of Michael

Van Valkenburgh Associates. "The technology is so new [in the United States] the exact lifespan is not actually confirmed yet."

A green roof regains open space lost as we establish cities and pave over countryside.

Green roofs, however, cost about twice as much to install, says Seattle's King County government in a 2004 study. The cost of green roofs is about $14 to $25 square foot. The higher cost and longer membrane life, however, appear to offset each other. The King-County study estimates that, over a 40-year life span, the "total costs of ownership for the green roof" is only about 10% higher than for a conventional roof design.

A green roof regains open space lost as we establish cities and pave over countryside. And with an alpine meadow on the roof, city dwellers can still enjoy a bit of nature.

The most common green roof in moderate climates (like Germany, which has used green roofs for over 30 years) is a single non-irrigated 3–4-inch layer of lightweight, compost soil with drought-resistant plants. The Germans find this kind of green roof gives the most benefit for the money; 14% of the new flat roofs in Germany are green roofs.

How Green Roofs Work

The main task for green roofs, like all roofs, is to protect the waterproof membrane from the elements to keep the roof from leaking. Well-designed green roofs come in layers to do three jobs:

Lower roof temperatures that, in the summer, can be extremely hot (130° F, 55° C). Lower temperatures and more even temperatures prolong the life of the waterproofing membrane by reducing heat damage and degradation.

Drain rainwater so any standing water doesn't damage the membrane, doesn't rot the plants, erode the soil system or cause the roof structure to sag under water weight.

Separate and protect the membrane from human feet on the rooftop and from plant roots (for example, stray tree seeds that have taken root).

The green-roof layers vary, depending on design, but all include:

Plants and soil—the top layer. Plants lower the waterproofing membrane temperature by absorbing 80% of the sun's radiation and using that energy to synthesize sugars and starches from carbon dioxide and water. The plants and soil also sponge up about 40% of the rain falling on the roof in a major 2-inch rainstorm, which reduces water flowing into storm sewers (more about this later).

A landscape or filter cloth to keep the soil from washing away. This layer separates the plant system from the rest of the roof. Also, many green roofs have walkways to protect the roof from foot-traffic wear.

Drainage layers that sometimes include built-in reservoirs. Plastic sheets, fabric or synthetic mats, or granular mineral layers are some of the drainage materials used to collect some of the water and allow the remainder to flow off. The main drainage design feature is, as with all roofs, a slightly sloping roof so gravity can move the water to the drains.

A root barrier (sometimes in the form of root repellant on the membrane) to block roots from penetrating the waterproofing membrane.

Below these layers come (not necessarily in this order) the waterproof membrane, insulation and the building structure—which must be especially strong to support the additional weight of the green roof. Sometimes . . . the insulation is placed above the waterproof membrane.

How Well They Function

The National Research Council of Canada (NRC) constructed a green-roof testing facility at its Ottawa campus. It consists of a roof area of about 800-square feet that's divided into two parts: one half with a bare waterproofing membrane on top and the other half with a green-roof covering the waterproof membrane. A wildflower meadow grows in six inches of lightweight soil. The Canadians instrumented both halves of the roof.

The University of Central Florida conducted a similar study, except comparing its green roof (6–8 inches of lightweight soil and a variety of native Florida vegetation) with a conventional roof surface. They, likewise divided a larger (3300-square foot) roof into two parts, and instrumented both halves.

The two groups found:

Green roofs modify temperature fluctuations of the membranes, thereby reducing thermal stress and possibly extending membrane life.

On a typical hot summer day in Ottawa, the outdoor temperature peaked at 95°F. The membrane on the Canadian reference roof reached 158° whereas the membrane on the green roof reached only about 77°F.

The Florida group found that "the maximum average day temperature for the conventional roof surface was 130°F while the maximum average day green roof surface temperature was 91°F—lower than the conventional roof." The average was measured over the period from July 4 to Sept. 1, 2005. . . .

Green roofs shade and insulate the roof and evaporate moisture. Thus, they cool the roof, and reduce the demand for air conditioning in the building below.

The Canadians found that, in the spring and, particularly, in the summer, the green roof reduced the average daily energy demand by up to 75%, compared with the reference roof.

The Floridians estimated that the average energy use to remove the additional heat gain from the conventional roof over the monitored summer period is approximately 700 watt-hours per day.

Green roofs delay runoff and reduce the runoff rate and volume. In a typical 12-hour period during a rainstorm, the Canadian green roof delayed runoff by about 45 minutes, and soaked up about 45% of the rain.

Green Roof Innovations

As an example of recent design improvements, consider the new green roof going up over the American Society of Landscape Architects (ASLA) building in Washington DC. The roof is a "matrix," says Stephen Noone of Michael Van Valkenburgh and Associates, the landscape architecture firm that is designing the green roof. An open space that people can stroll and sit on overlays a regular green roof.

Green roofs help city environments.

More innovations: a metal grating that "floats" about three inches over the greenery and soil, says Counts. The architects hope that plants will grow up through the grating, and then people, walking on the plants, will give the plants a "haircut", which regenerates the plants. Also the architects will put the waterproofing down first, then cover with rigid insulation. The reason, explains Counts, is so the "various elements, such as deck and the metal grating, will sit or bear on the rigid insulation rather the waterproof membrane as in the traditional system." This protects the membrane from rubbing caused by shifting movements in the waves, deck and metal grating as the construction crew builds the elements and as people "occupy the roof." Finally, they plan to construct greenery-covered "waves" made of foam, and shaped to create a valley-like place to stroll.

Green Roofs and the Environment

Yes, green roofs help city environments. In addition to improving the environment of a single building, as we've discussed, they also improve the environment of a city. That's the reason the German government gave green roofs a big push. "Over 77 German municipalities invest in green roofs," says Elevated Landscape Technologies of Brantfort, Ontario, Canada. As German cities got larger, municipal governments started to tax property owners for releasing storm water from their properties. "This has been the largest driver in creating the developed green-roof industry in Europe."

Why? Because green roofs cut runoff from roofs by about 40%, and also delay the flow from roofs about 45 minutes. Both actions help city storm sewers cope with a storm runoff. If rain swamps a sewer's capacity, then storm sewage overflows in the city.

Other benefits are more speculative. "If widely adopted, rooftop gardens could reduce the urban heat island, which would decrease smog episodes . . ." says Karen Liu of the NRC. Plants ". . . can also filter out airborne pollutants washed off in the rain, thus improving the quality of the runoff," she adds. A study done by Weston Design Consultants for Chicago estimates that the greening of all of that city's rooftops would cut peak power demand for air conditioning by 720 megawatts— which is the equivalent of several coal-fired generating stations or one small nuclear power plant.

12

Green Architecture Requires Good Design

Cathleen McGuigan

Cathleen McGuigan is the National Arts Correspondent for Newsweek, *covering books, theater, design, and culture.*

Green architecture has been promoted as an environmentally friendly development, but the reality has often been less than promised. Because green architecture frequently places practicality above beauty, these buildings have often been aesthetically unattractive. Green designs have also proven to have an environmental downside. For instance, while Las Vegas plans for green resorts, tourists traveling to Las Vegas still require jets and jet fuel. A number of established architects have learned to incorporate innovative design with green features, but this is the exception, not the rule. Until architects learn to accept green design as a standard practice, green architecture will continue to fall short of its promise.

I hate green architecture. I can't stand the hype, the marketing claims, the smug lists of green features that supposedly transform a garden-variety new building into a structure fit for Eden. Grassy roofs? Swell! Recycled gray water to flush the toilets? Excellent! But if 500 employees have to drive 40 miles a day to work in the place—well, how green is that? Achieving real sustainability is much more complicated than the publicity suggests. And that media roar is only getting louder. The urge to build green is exploding: more than 16,000 projects are now registered with the U.S. Green Building Council as intending to go for a LEED (Leadership in Energy and Environmental Design)—or sustainable—certification, up from just 573 in 2000.

When it comes to green, people don't want to hear that size matters.

Among those are various plans to build at least 50 million square feet of new green resorts in Las Vegas, where ecoconsciousness is suddenly as hot as Texas Hold 'Em. The largest LEED-rated building in the country is the 8.3 million-square-foot Palazzo Resort Hotel and Casino, which opened there last January. As it happens, the state of Nevada offers developers property-tax rebates—up to 35 percent—for LEED certification. Don't worry about the tons of jet fuel that will be used to deliver millions more tourists to Vegas each year—those visitors can help make up for that by reusing the towels in their hotels.

"Green McMansions"

When it comes to green, people don't want to hear that size matters. We keep building not just bigger entertainment complexes but bigger houses. "Green McMansion" is one of my favorite oxymorons. Currently the average new house is 2,500 square feet, up 1.5 percent in size from last year—though the shock of this winter's fuel bills may finally slow the trend. Building green houses—or at least advertising them as green—is on the rise, though there are no national standards about what constitutes a green home. People are attracted to sustainable houses partly as a cool novelty, when in fact green dwellings have been around for eons. Think of igloos, tepees or yurts—they took advantage of readily available local materials and were designed to suit their specific environments.

Shelters around the world tend to be situated to benefit from the sun in the winter or to shield their inhabitants from chilling winds. But we forgot those basic principles when we plunked down every possible style of house into our sprawling American suburbs.

If you want to understand what makes sustainable sense, check out the classic old shotgun houses of New Orleans that best survived Katrina (and just got a pass from Gustav): these modest homes are built high off the ground to resist flood damage; they are made of local wood that dries out; they have high ceilings and cross ventilation to deal with the stifling summer heat. But the houses that were ruined—whether in the Lower Ninth Ward or more-affluent neighborhoods—tended to be low-slung ranch houses, a style originally developed for the climate of California.

Innovative Green Designs

What bugs me most about the fad for green architecture is the notion that virtue makes for better design. OK, I suppose an ugly green building is better than an ugly nongreen building—but it's still ugly. So when I come upon a beautiful sustainable building that doesn't scream green, it cheers me up. The California Academy of Sciences, opening later this month in San Francisco, is a perfect example. It replaces the old science museum that was damaged in the 1989 Loma Prieta earthquake. Its design is sensitive to its place and history: the new building doesn't gobble up more space on its spectacular site in Golden Gate Park, and its architect, Renzo Piano, was careful to go no higher—36 feet—than the original structure. The most obvious ecofeature of his elegantly simple glass-sided pavilion is the green roof: a rolling 2.5-acre terrain, inspired in part by the surrounding hills, it cleverly disguises, under its two biggest bumps, the domes of the planetarium and of the rainforest exhibit underneath. The roof is planted with 40 native species (unlike Golden Gate Park itself, which was created out of a sand pit and includes such glamorous nonnatives as palm trees). The plants are kind of low and scrubby—though they bloom at various times—but they were chosen less for prettiness than hardiness, and the fact that they won't need irrigation.

For the next generation of architects, sustainability will be second nature.

There are lots of examples of innovative green technology in the building, but perhaps the most surprising is in the museum's offices where, says the executive director, Gregory Farrington, you can see hardware that's rare in today's buildings: handles to open the windows. That's because, amazingly, there's no artificial cool air. The only air conditioning is provided free of charge by the breezes that blow off the Pacific—including those that are naturally pulled down by that curvy roof into a lovely open piazza at the center of the museum. "It's a building that breathes with nature," says Piano. And all the gizmos that make this building even greener—the weather sensors that dim or brighten the artificial lights; the thousands of little solar cells tucked into the roof overhangs; the old denim jeans recycled as insulation—are so carefully integrated into the overall architecture that you hardly notice them. Of course, the green features will be explained in the museum's education programs—each year, 50,000 San Francisco schoolkids will visit its aquarium, alligator pool and other exhibits of the living and the dead. But personally, I like that Piano's trademark gifts for inventive design and great craftsmanship seem to make the sustainable elements disappear. "Making green buildings is a practical answer," he says in the accent of his native Italy. "But architecture is about desire; it's about dreams."

The Green Technology Future

Spoken like a true romantic, but the point is right-on: sustainability is about the practical systems of building, not the beauty of great design. Established architects like Piano—he's 71—have learned to integrate green into their practices, depending on where they're working (the rules are strict in many countries of Europe, where Piano is based). But for the next generation of architects, sustainability will be second nature—they're learning in architecture schools how to incorporate green into design, and some of them will become the innovators who'll devise ever more efficient ecological solutions. And the U.S. Green Building Council is continuing to evolve its suggested standards: access to mass transit, rather than the necessity of cars, gets credit, as does adapting to a specific climate—a principle central to the sustainability of the California Academy of Sciences. It's expected to score a LEED platinum rating, making it the greenest museum in the United States. But I wish we didn't have to trumpet that achievement in the same breath as praising its design. I look forward to a future when green architecture won't be discretionary but required of every architect and builder. Then we could all shut up about it. Sustainable features would become as exciting as the plumbing systems and as essential as a roof that keeps out the rain.

13

Green Cities Must Serve People Instead of Cars

Richard Register

Richard Register is the President of Ecocity Builders of Oakland, California, and the author of Ecocities: Building Cities in Balance with Nature.

Many environmentalists have continued to believe that they can maintain an automobile dependent society by creating "greener" fuel or greener cars. Unfortunately, this strategy is misguided. Simply put, the entire urban system—automobiles, highways, and suburbs—is not sustainable. New environmentally-friendly cities need to be built. These green cities will grow upward, accomodating more people in limited space and allowing the outlying reaches of suburban sprawl to revert to farmland. Green cities will house people nearer to places of work, allowing for walking and bicycling. Transforming traditional cities into green cities will not be an easy task, but it is the only real solution to the current environmental crisis.

Over the past century, our cities have been shaped— literally—for the benefit of the automobile and oil industries. Today, with global oil reserves headed toward irreversible decline, we need to face the challenges of the imminent post-oil reality. Seizing foreign oil fields . . . will not solve our environmental problems. Building Green Cities for people, not cars, will.

In their controversial essay, "The Death of Environmentalism," Michael Shellenberger and Ted Nordhaus claim that the

Richard Register, "Green Cities and the End of the Age of Oil," *Energy Bulletin*, August 24, 2005. Reproduced by permission.

environmental movement has worked its way into historical irrelevance. These writers suggest that "the greatest tragedy of the 1990s is that, in the end, the environmental community had still not come up with an inspiring vision, much less a legislative proposal, that the majority of Americans could get excited about."

The private automobile is still part of an unsustainable urban system that requires massive networks of streets, freeways, and parking structures to serve congested cities and far-flung suburbs.

I disagree, not only with these two green movement morticians but also with some of their critics. Carl Pope, executive director of the Sierra Club, has rightly scolded Shellenberger and Nordhaus for "failing to offer their own ideas," a lapse that "rendered their report nihilistic—able to destroy but not create." But what does Pope offer? The environmental movement, he says, "needs deeper, more robust, more sustained collaborations" and "a new economic order." His action plan is focused on renewable energy. Does he see any alternative to tacking solar panels onto the past century's exoskeleton of freeways, automobiles and sprawl? Not in his response. "As early as the Carter Administration," Pope writes, "the Sierra Club sought an alliance with the United Auto Workers . . . to preserve and enhance the U.S. auto industry." In their desire to deliver "what Mainstream America wants," environmentalists discovered that people wanted cars. So the Sierra Club's response has been to try and convince the auto industry that the environmental situation could be improved if Detroit simply built a "better" automobile. This won't work and here's why.

The 'Green Car' Myth

Consider the energy required to move a 130-pound human body by foot as compared to moving that same body the same distance seated behind the wheel of a 4,000-pound SUV. The average human can hit about 5 miles-per-hour in a brisk walk while the typical car averages 40 mph (city and freeway). While it is true that you can move eight times faster inside a two-ton vehicle, accomplishing this feat requires burning around 1,900 times as much energy (and that's not factoring in friction, which increases with speed). This should tell you something about the fundamental insanity of depending on gas-fueled cars in an oil-starved future.

And, it's not just the oil. Even if powered by biodiesel, hydrogen or sunbeams the private automobile is still part of an unsustainable urban system that requires massive networks of streets, freeways, and parking structures to serve congested cities and far-flung suburbs. Driving a Prius hybrid simply makes it easier for people to live farther from the rest of their lives (while seducing them into thinking that they are "doing something for the environment"). We don't want to face this truth because it implies too much change. Autoworkers want to keep their jobs and Sierra Clubers want to be free to drive 40 miles to experience nature whenever they feel like it.

Raised in a car-worshiping culture, we tend to assume that everyone lives in a world of breezy trips through city streets and top-down forays deep into the country. It's hard to believe there are worlds without cars. But the startling fact is that, far from being a majority, only one of thirteen people on Earth actually owns a car. Consider this: 92 percent of the world's people do not own cars—and the 8 percent who do are directly responsible for climate change and the alarming collapse of biodiversity on planet Earth.

If the auto industry is to have any future in a post-oil world, it may have to retrain its workers to build the efficient mass-transit systems that will serve the new ecologically healthy Green Cities, towns and villages of the 21st century. Environmentalists and autoworkers should begin thinking hard about how to rebuild low-energy, car-free cities. Auto-workers should be studying renewable energy systems and lobbying for massive federal investments in those technologies. We need to rebuild our entire civilization (towns and villages, too) on this basis. A proper accounting of the auto-urban paradigm would include the energy needed to draw the oil, cook the asphalt, erect the freeways, mine and mill the steel used to manufacture the cars and, of course, deploy the troops and weaponry to secure America's access to foreign oil. Add it all up and you begin to get a sense of the enormity of the problem.

Of course, it's a hard assignment. How could solving a problem as large as preventing the collapse of planetary biodiversity and inventing a new civilization in balance with nature be an easy task?

How Cars Shape Cities

The oil-burning, fume-spewing private automobile is only part of a larger environmentally damaging system—the energy-intensive spawling infrastructure of our cities. When small buildings are scattered over large areas, more energy is required for heating and cooling as well as for transportation. Pedestrian-friendly Green Cities—built for people, bicycles, mass transit and renewable energy—would not only cut air pollution, they also would promote the rebuilding of essential soil and water resources while increasing plant and animal biodiversity.

Knowledgeable environmentalists extol the Leadership in Energy and Environmental Design (LEED) standards for buildings, but they seldom apply similar standards to cities. Last summer, I was a speaker at a Sustainable Communities Conference in Vermont. The organizers took two busloads of participants to admire a beautiful new LEED platinum-rated factory that produces towers for wind electric generators. Hard to get greener that that.

But there was a problem: it took us 20 minutes on the highway to get there. And, when we arrived, there was no other building in sight on the rolling landscape of broad agricultural fields.

"Wouldn't it be more fun," I asked the company tour guide, "if instead of driving way out to this splendid isolation and back every day, you could just walk out the factory door and bike over to a class or back to your residence?" Here was a beautifully designed solar building with state-of-the-art natural lighting and insulation, constructed so the residents would consume almost no energy—except for the hundreds of gallons of gasoline they burned in their cars every day to get there!

The Eco-City Vision

"No wonder the public doesn't want to hear the truth about global warming," former Sierra Club President Adam Werbach laments, "Nobody's offering them a vision for the future that matches the magnitude of the problem."

Excuse me? Dozens of environmental thinkers have been offering such a vision for 30 years. I've co-produced five international Eco-City conferences on five continents, written three books and been invited to speak on every continent.

Like Pope, Werbach calls for renewable energy. Good idea, but not enough. The renewable energy regime needs a physical infrastructure in which to operate—i.e., a city to match. If you install a fleet of clean, solar-powered buses in a typical sprawling low-density city, those "eco-buses" are still going to run practically empty. Rebuilding cities for pedestrians will reverse sprawl by bringing departure points and destinations closer together. City planners call this "mixed use" and "balanced development." Freeways could slowly be torn down as pedestrian-friendly cities are efficiently—and affordably—

connected by train. That's a vision worth adopting. But, in order for this to happen, environmentalists and developers need to work together.

How to Build Eco-Cities

The first step toward turning today's Gridlocked Cities into Green Cities is to identify the major commercial and neighborhood centers and map them for higher density. Re-zoning to facilitate higher-density pedestrian transit centers will promote "access by proximity—instead of transportation." As these centralized pedestrian/transit centers grow in density and diversity, outlying areas would be replaced by natural areas, open spaces, and small farms.

The ecological Green City would be alive with bicycles, solar greenhouses, creeks, plants, animals, and people.

Metropolitan areas now spread over (hundreds of) thousands of acres need to break up into discrete communities— forming archipelagos of smaller, compact Green Cities around what are today's downtowns. Ecovillages would arise where today's neighborhood centers now exist. In his classic book, Ecotopia, Berkeley author Ernest Callenbach envisioned the Bay Area metropolis (which includes Oakland, San Jose, Berkeley, Palo Alto and Richmond) transforming into a necklace of separate towns linked by high-speed public transportation—each with its own particular economy, products and character (and all surrounded by resurgent green and edged by the shimmering waters of San Francisco Bay).

A Transfer of Development Rights (TDR) offers one promising tool for facilitating the transitions required by ecological city design. A developer can use a TDR to purchase and remove a building whose crumbling foundation sits atop a buried creek. In return, the developer wins the privilege of erecting a larger building in a pedestrian/transit center. The developer gets a "density bonus" and the city gains new open space for a community garden, public park, or sports field and more housing in transit/pedestrian centers.

But won't it be oppressive to live in more densely settled core cities? Not if you build them with lots of sun pouring into the interiors, heating and refreshing the air without the use of fossil fuels or nuclear fission. Build rooftop gardens, cafes, promenades, mini-parks, entertainment enclaves and recreation outposts high in the buildings to provide spectacular views overlooking the city's reviving bioregion. Solar collectors and windmills would glint in the sun. The ecological Green City would be alive with bicycles, solar greenhouses, creeks, plants, animals, and people.

Car-Free Zones

Builders of the new housing units in these evolving Green Cities would recruit renters and condo owners who wished to free themselves from cars. Contrary to legend, there are many such people out there. Businesses would grant hiring preference to people living nearby. Given sufficient diversity, you don't need to travel far for life's basics: shelter, job, school, food. Green City buildings could be interlinked by high bridges so that clusters of structures become easily available to pedestrians on many levels. Terraces with communal gardens would provide fresh produce and rooftop parks would provide recreation—all accessible by glass elevators gliding over the outsides of buildings offering stunning views of the new vertical Green City environment.

Eco Cities would promote the restoration of ancient creeks buried under pavement and concrete.

Facilities needing little natural light (theaters, photolabs, warehouses) would be located in the lower stories, lifting other downtown activities higher into the sun. Covered streets would have the grandeur of cathedrals (with beams of light falling into quiet interiors bustling with pedestrians). Downtown buildings would provide workplaces for residents. The hundreds of thousands who once poured into the city over miles of freeways, would now quietly zip to work on foot or bicycle leaving a minority of outside workers to arrive by bus and rail.

First we'd create car-free streets, then larger, car-free zones. As any tourist returning from a European vacation can testify, car-free streets and plazas are extremely pleasant community enclaves that bristle with life and are economically self-sustaining.

A Lasting Environmental Solution

Eco Cities would promote the restoration of ancient creeks buried under pavement and concrete. Living streams, shore-fronts, wetlands, and ridgelines would once again become signature landmarks for Green City residents. Restored urban creeks and wooded groves would provide natural habitat for birds and animals and become beautiful and educational local resources for Green City children who would no longer need to climb into a car and drive 40 miles to "experience nature." With sufficient care, restored creeks magically reawaken with populations of dragonflies, butterflies, hummingbirds, fish, and crawdads. In California, native salmon and large wading birds like egrets and herons have already returned to some of these reborn watersheds.

Rebuilding our cities to serve people, not cars, will take decades, but the transformation offers lasting solutions for most of our most pressing environmental problems. These solutions will start to appear immediately. They will multiply rapidly as the transformation proceeds.

14

Sensible Urban Growth Is Achievable

Anthony Flint

Anthony Flint is a journalist and author at the Lincoln Institute of Land Policy.

The American city is defined by sprawl, the result of poor planning and little foresight. Everything in the American urban environment—homes, garages, and SUVs—is super-sized. In the near future as populations grow quickly, a new, smart growth vision of urban space will have to be realized. While smart growth is often seen as a progressive idea, it is actually conservative: smart growth can save urban dwellers money in the long run. Developers should be allowed to further develop dense urban spaces instead of building outward and outdated zoning laws— laws regulating building—should be revamped. For smart growth to work, individuals will also have to get involved, learning to live in smaller houses, choosing to walk or ride a bike instead of drive, and becoming active within their communities. Individual consumers will ultimately have the power to transform suburban sprawl into green communities of the future.

Andrés Duany was on vacation in the little Cape Cod town of Mashpee when he passed by the fire station and saw a long, muscular ladder truck parked out front, all gleaming with chrome and glossy red paint and gold letters on the side. The bright white extending ladder looked like it could go

Anthony Flint, *This Land: The Battle Over Sprawl and the Future of America*. Baltimore, MD: John Hopkins University Press, 2006. Copyright ©: 2006 The Johns Hopkins University Press.

pretty high—and, sure enough, a fire apparatus expert on the Cape identifies the vehicle on his website as a 2001 Pierce Dash 2000/3000, able to extend 100 feet into the air. Put into service in 2001, it is Mashpee's "first aerial device," the website says. There's only one thing. There are church steeples and cats caught in towering oak trees from time to time, but the tallest buildings in Mashpee are no more than three stories high, and there are only a handful of those.

Duany, the New Urbanism [a design philosophy promoting workable neighborhoods] founder, asked a local developer involved in Mashpee Commons, a compact shopping village built on an old strip mall site in the middle of the town, why the fire department had the big ladder truck. There was one main reason, the developer replied. The local firefighters get paid more money for operating such equipment—the heavier and more complicated the equipment, the higher the pay.

The long ladder truck has a ripple effect, however. The streets in Mashpee's developments must all be wide enough for the big emergency vehicles to navigate. That means the wide, looping streets common in cul-de-sac subdivisions and not the narrow, grid-based streets that New Urbanism and more compact development call for. Trucking firms, parcel delivery companies, and the U.S. Postal Service follow the fire department's lead, because they also all like streets to be wide. Over time the generous street layouts have become codified in the local planning and zoning process. They are not just desired but required. Developers adopt them in standardized subdivision plans—one less detail to worry about for them. But any developer trying to build something more compact has to go through a special permit process, something that costs time and money and dissuades most builders in the first place. Spread-out residential development with lots of asphalt is the result.

City Sprawl

Call it the chaos theory of sprawl. The fluttering of a butterfly's wings [the action that starts a ripple effect] in this case is the local firefighters' union, leading to the storm of wide streets and low-density development that future generations are now stuck with.

For something so primary—something we see every day, something that dictates how we live and function, that has such direct influence on our attitudes and moods—the American landscape is shaped with very little intention. The guiding principle for arranging the physical environment isn't feng shui [Chinese aesthetic principles for organizing one's surroundings]. It's non sequitur [non-logical response].

And in the absence of more thoughtful design and planning, the default setting is big. It's super-sized. While the average home interior is about 2,500 square feet, McMansions, starter castles, and garage mahals [after Taj Mahal] are in the 3,000- to 4,000-square-foot range. Our garages are getting bigger to accommodate bigger SUVs and protruding in such a way that they earn the moniker "snout house." We fit out our private, interior realm with great care and expertise, but the exterior world is mostly an afterthought. The chief requirements are wide roads that lead to the commercial strips and the highway on-ramp for the commute to work, and maybe some shrubs around the low-slung sign that announces the subdivision community and acts as a de facto gate.

In Pasco County, Florida, near Tampa, KB Homes does painstaking marketing surveys to determine what people want—things like a sense of safety, the maximum acceptable commute time, or a backyard view with privacy. What KB Homes doesn't talk about is how the commute may start out at half an hour but will become much longer as more people move in. The homebuyers aren't asked if they're really prepared for three-figure monthly energy bills, or to spend thousands on maintaining the two cars necessary to get around, and who knows how much in gasoline costs. They aren't warned that they will end up paying higher taxes very soon to pay for police and fire protection and the extension of water and sewer infrastructure to support the ever-expanding exurbia.

And yet subdivisions like the ones in Pasco County just keep coming, in Little Elm outside Dallas, around Mesa near Phoenix, all around Boise, Idaho, all through northern New Jersey and central Massachusetts, and all over the fields and farmland of Ohio and Maryland and Pennsylvania—over and over and over again.

Smart growth saves money through a more efficient use of existing infrastructure.

Stopping Urban Sprawl

Remember those 100 million new people expected in the country by 2050? They're the reason we're going to need more compact places. If the development patterns just keep going out in a straight line, we're going to have a series of 100-mile-wide, dysfunctional metropolitan areas, all going broke trying to pay for infrastructure and basic services, dealing with road rage from continual traffic jams, and home to children who are even fatter and less active than they are today. That's not a future suitable for the dignity of America.

What will make the difference is more choice, not less. The smart growth movement has tried to broadcast this message with a kind of civic guerrilla warfare. But there's a bigger idea at the movement's disposal.

Smart growth is a conservative idea.

Smart growth saves money through a more efficient use of existing infrastructure. State governments are going to have to exercise fiscal discipline more than ever in the years ahead, especially to avoid increases in taxes. Smart growth is conservative as well because it preserves what we have, whether existing open space or historical sites. And at its best smart growth gets government out of the way of the free market. Zoning that has been amended and calcified over the past eighty years is a senseless barrier and impediment to developers trying new things and building in urban places. Clearing that underbrush is ultimately on of conservatism's primary acts: cutting regulation for business. The subsidies inherent in the country's post-World War II framework for development are just the kind of exercise in government picking winners and losers that conservatives abhor.

It may seem counterintuitive, but the answer to runaway development is more development.

Getting government out of the way is a big theme in the first two healthy habits on this list, which is the result of years of reporting on and thinking about development in America. There are several ways in which the anti-sprawl movement can better concentrate its fire, prompting policy changes that will open the door for big changes in attitude about how we live.

Let Builders Build

It may seem counterintuitive, but the answer to runaway development is more development. In the areas that are already built up, that is. Developers know that diverse, multifamily, mixed-use projects on urban infill parcels are the wave of the future. They've already targeted the land. That's what smart growth calls for. But the builders are having a tough time, with outdated codes and onerous, time-consuming, and sometimes contradictory bureaucratic procedures. At the same time, NIMBYism [Not In My Back Yard] puts fearful residents in an automatic defensive mode. They are not being shown a context and a bigger picture. The twin barriers of red tape and neighborhood resistance make developers give up just when their efforts are needed most. Advocacy groups need to stop making it worse by nitpicking projects. In my hometown of South Boston, it took years for builders of three major residential towers to get approvals. The haggling was over the height of the towers and the size of a planned park and dozens of other issues. By the time it was over, the developers had missed the economic cycle. As I gaze out my window to the development site, there's still nothing there. Those hundreds of new residences would have been mostly luxury units, but they would have added to the overall housing stock (and tax base) in Boston and taken some of the pricing pressure off neighborhoods like Dorchester and Jamaica Plain. The site is a vacant lot near a new transit line—a vacant lot, right beside Boston Harbor. The developers could have built to the heavens, it was such a sensible spot for growth. They should have been welcomed with open arms.

Emphasizing growth in already built-up settings—promoting the reuse of vacant lots, cleaning up brownfield industrial sites—is a kind of supply-side approach. It's better for smart growth's image than dwelling on restrictions in the countryside. And the appeal of city living is self-propagating. Millions will still live in sprawl, but the advantages of city living—the culture, the diversity, the baseball field a short walk from home—reveal themselves powerfully. Cities have a great running start, with their infrastructure and sense of place—a big attraction for businesses that care about employees' quality of life. As for the technology that, some say, makes cities irrelevant? Harness it with free wireless hotspots in parks and public spaces, to make it easy both to be untethered and to have personal interactions. Multiuse pathways that promote physical activity, historic and contemporary architecture that inspires creativity—there's not a single amenity cities can't provide that's better than the suburbs, as long as developers are allowed to be the engine of growth and improvement.

Abolish Zoning as We Know It

Throw it out. Start over. Conventional zoning is full of sense-less loopholes and grandfather clauses. It's based on an out-dated planning philosophy—the separation of uses—from the 1920s. What else in this country do we stake on ideas from nearly a century ago, let alone something as important as the physical landscape? With the exception of baseball, rules are meant to evolve over time. But zoning has been amended and patched and added on to in such a convoluted way that it's better to make a fresh start.

Zoning written in the 1920s, largely in response to public health concerns that prompted a segregation of residential, commercial, and industrial functions, makes more compact living impossible in America today. Multifamily housing is outlawed in many communities. As Douglas Foy, Massachu-setts Governor Mitt Romney's development chief, puts it, "You can't build a Concord today," referring to the traditional New England town center northwest of Boston. "It's illegal."

Even a targeted overhaul of zoning would help, smoothing the way for new approaches like residences over ground-floor retail, which either is impossible today or else requires a diffi-cult special permit. Pointless bans on mixed-use districts or multifamily housing should be lifted. Sprawl-inducing provi-sions like "approval not required" could be eliminated if de-velopers were given something better—the chance to build more housing in town centers, through a multitown system of development-rights trading and tax-revenue sharing.

New Urbanism's SmartCode [a unified land development ordinance template] is worth looking at, although maintaining transect—the six zones of settlement—arguably might require replacing one set of rigid requirements with another. The key is to open up the possibilities so that building in the right places isn't so hard. Changing the framework and the rules of the development game by replacing outdated zoning creates more options instead of constantly closing them down. Single-family, detached homes would of course still be allowed. But they wouldn't be the *only* thing that's allowed, which is pretty much the case with most conventional zoning. Suburban developers are playing with the rules stacked in their favor, so there's no real competition in the marketplace. That should be anathema to conservatives. How can anyone say that consumers don't like New Urbanism if it can't even be built?

Be Your Own Makeover Artist

We're demanding good design in all kinds of products, from home appliances to cars, in what has been called a "Beatles moment"—reflecting tastes that are both sophisticated and popular. We're spending a lot of time watching HGTV and redoing our basements and closets. Why not take it a step further and reevaluate our choice of living circumstances on a grander scale?

There should be a consumer revolt about the entire process of development in America.

An honest self-test can tell you if a 4,000-square-foot home in a subdivision is really worth the trade-offs of a long commute and time away from the kids. You might find that you need less space than you think. The "right-sizing" craze—the quest for a streamlined, more simplified life—has not gone unnoticed by the likes of the Container Store, jam-packed with folks trying to get organized. You might find being more efficient in terms of *where* you live pays even more dividends: saving money on gas, walking more, and living in a more diverse and compact village-like setting. You'll feel healthier. You'll be part of a community. When the outside world is as nice as the private, interior realm, your mood doesn't change when you walk out the door.

It's fine if you conclude those things aren't so important and you end up in a subdivision. But the choice shouldn't be automatic. I'm surprised there isn't more resentment among independent-minded Americans at the way conventional homebuilders steer consumers toward one product—and increasingly a product with shoddy workmanship, a by-product of rapid-fire construction. (Architecture critic Ada Louise Huxtable famously asked an Italian worker how it was possible to erect buildings so quickly. "Senza rispetto" was the response—without respect.)

There should be a consumer revolt about the entire process of development in America. It creates the illusion that the homebuyer is in the driver's seat. Once more people realize that's not the case, there's nothing more powerful than a ticked-off consumer. A major real estate company ran a commercial that showed a competitor driving a couple around, who said they wanted a Tudor. But the agent just kept pulling into driveway after driveway of identical split-level ranches. The housing marketplace can be a lot like that, with developers and financial institutions keeping buyers stuck in the rut of the detached single-family subdivision home.

The smart developers already understand both the rapidly changing American demographic and the dead-end nature of sprawling out farther and farther into the countryside. Their focus on urban land started years ago. They know they have to cater to a marketplace of niches—older people who don't want to drive, young professionals, frustrated solo drivers looking for shorter commutes. Stop and think whether you might be one of those people.

The smart growth and New Urbanism movements should keep up their end of the bargain by respecting what people truly want, like the obvious need for most families to own a car. They shouldn't oversell—like saying compact development *automatically* promotes a sense of community or makes you physically fit—and they shouldn't lecture. Any new rules and restrictions to guide development should have the hallmarks of flexibility and fairness, with respect for property rights, the free market, and personal choice.

Suburban towns that developed in the 1950s and 1960s . . . might need more work, but they still have lots of potential.

Behold the Older Suburb

Just as the answer to unchecked development is more development, the solution to suburbia lies with the suburbs. Not the sprawling ex-urban expanses of Little Elm or Santa Clarita, but what Douglas Kelbaugh, dean of the architecture school at the University of Michigan, calls the "Chesterfield" suburbs— the first generation of suburbs, from before the turn of the century to World War II. A college classmate of mine, Anne Gustafson, says she and other professional families have settled happily in Pelham, New York, in Westchester County, as an alternative to both the city and more leafy suburbia farther afield. The parents are all active in the schools, volunteer groups tend to the parks and public spaces, and it's minutes by train to Manhattan. Rediscovering this kind of place— passed over in the rush to the outer fringe—is an exemplary use of already built-up areas that have infrastructure and are convenient to employment centers and in most cases have a thriving Main Street-style downtown.

Some of these suburbs are absurdly expensive, whether Brookline and Newton outside Boston, parts of Westchester County outside New York, or Oak Park outside Chicago. But the concept of older suburbs doesn't have to be limited. Suburban towns that developed in the 1950s and 1960s—yes, even those that might be accused of being the start of sprawl— might need more work, but they still have lots of potential. They have tree-lined streets and sidewalks and lots with little yards, struggling downtowns and town centers, and often a commuter rail station. They have what planners call good bones.

Randolph, Massachusetts, is one such "first-ring" suburb, and it's struggling with a diverse population, fiscal problems, and a sketchy housing stock. But some of these little towns remind me of the urban neighborhoods that have been so famously revitalized.

Immigrants long ago discovered older suburbs and small cities outside the urban core. I found myself in Maynard, Massachusetts, on an assignment several years ago and noticed Brazilian restaurants and travel agents and supermarkets. I returned to do a story on the phenomenon: sure enough, Brazilian immigrants had moved into Maynard and Framingham and Lynn, taking advantage of lower home prices and the convenience of being close to Boston. They skipped the traditional stop in Boston itself and headed to these established places outside the big city. As I discovered, that's happening all over the country, making older suburbs more diverse than they ever were in the 1950s. And the foreign-born are only one part of the mix: there are gay older suburbs and hip and professional older suburbs, anything but your grandfather's first-ring suburb. They are an ideal middle landscape, and hundreds are just waiting to be transformed, like the now-chic urban neighborhoods before them. They are halfway to everywhere, in the words of the former mayor of Indianapolis.

Radical change in the public school system is the only way the middle class will ever return to urban America.

Reinventing older suburbs is an act of recycling, rather than constantly building new places in the countryside. But their best attributes for homebuyers are convenience and a retro feel. It may soon be as hip to live in Montclair, South-field, Bellaire, and Burbank as in Park Slope or on the Lower East Side.

Getting Involved

But not just to fight things. The secret to success in older sub-urbs and in cities is not just what people do with their homes and lots but the activism of residents reaching out in the broader community—getting involved in maintaining parks and playgrounds and, perhaps most critically, the school sys-tem. There is nothing more powerful than an engaged con-stituency to bring new ideas and vigorous thinking to the en-trenched bureaucracy of a public school. Demand innovation and a sharp break from the failed practices of the past, whether it's neighborhood schools that bust free of outdated assign-ment plans or pilot schools with principals who have a free hand in administration. Radical change in the public school system is the only way the middle class will ever return to ur-ban America. The same is true for many older suburbs.

Remember the "visioning" sessions in Salt Lake City and Chicago? Similar efforts are under way from Boston to Port-land. Sign up for them. There's great technology available to-day for creating a "futures" database, which shows what the community will look like in twenty years should current de-velopment patterns continue. If citizens don't like what they see, they can plug in some changes, like modifying zoning to allow more density in town centers. They can then see, for ex-ample, what will happen to home prices, which in turn affect the kind of workforce their region can attract, and in turn what kind of businesses. It's easy to peek behind the curtain and understand the many factors that weave together to create the landscapes we all have to deal with every day.

A little understanding leads to civic innovation and to grassroots campaigns that encourage government to think outside the box. The local transit agency should be involved in not just trains and buses but also the development of parking lots at stations. Your governor should feel free to reorganize state government—for example, coordinating the agencies responsible for transportation, housing, the environment energy, and economic development—to halt the mindless subsidy of sprawl through annual infrastructure funding. Even small changes in the framework of that spending—so much of which goes on behind the scenes—can make a big difference. South Carolina Governor Mark Sanford's elimination of minimum acreage requirements for new schools may seem like a minor bureaucratic adjustment, but it made the entire state rethink where schools are best located. Support a law that requires state institutions like prisons and schools to buy from local farms, or a change in tax policy that bases value on land instead of buildings. It's the fine print of state and local government and it can be tedious and technical, but that's where the action is.

Today being involved in development decisions for most Americans means showing up at a public meeting and criticizing projects that have been proposed down the street. It doesn't have to be that way. The energy can be redirected. If we understand the details and the logic behind good design, use technology to become citizen planners, and extend our extreme-makeover expertise from our closets to the community at large, there will be no stopping the excellence that Americans will create in the landscape.

Demand a Better Discourse

At my desk in the newsroom of the *Boston Globe*, I took a plaintive call from the head of a regional planning agency, trying to get coverage of one of those visioning sessions. What will it take for the *Globe* to cover this, he asked. Arrange to have a small dog get stuck in a culvert outside the meeting hall, I advised, and have one of your planners pull the pooch to safety.

The response was tongue-in-cheek, of course. But with a few notable exceptions—the *Washington Post, USA Today*, the *Detroit Free-Press*, the *Cincinnati Enquirer*, or the *Newark Star-Ledger*—the media aren't terribly interested in covering planning and development or posing big questions about a region's future. There's much more interest in scheduled press conferences, crime, and politicians and business leaders caught with their hands in the cookie jar. When growth does get covered, the dots aren't connected. The business section runs a story on the opening of a big mall, and the metro section writes about residents complaining about traffic jams in the area a few months later. Indeed, there is a conscious effort not to try to connect any dots. After ten years of providing stories and perspectives about development in the fast-growing region, the *Atlanta Journal-Constitution* killed its Horizons section in 2005 and reassigned its reporters to conventional beats. An editor once told me my stories about growth were too "reflective."

The smart growth movement recognizes the futility of lecturing to the American people

---

The mainstream media, of course, are in an energetic and slightly panicky quest to be interesting, to stave off even more massive defections to the Internet. I happen to think there's an appetite for probing stories about growth as well as the latest on Martha Stewart or a restaurant review. But there are other factors at work. After years of accusations of a liberal bias in the media, fewer journalists have the stomach to be critical of red-state, suburban America. They don't want to be seen as taking sides with environmentalists or equity planners or any one in the smart growth camp. Editors worry about even using the terms "smart growth" and "sprawl." They strive for balance, giving equal time to global warming skeptics and creationists alike. But in the process some critical questions aren't being asked.

Citizens should demand more of their media. They should call for major projects on what the region will look like in twenty years and daily coverage that doesn't just focus on neighbors calling each other names at zoning meetings. Their intelligence shouldn't be under estimated. A more thoughtful discourse will in turn embolden politicians and civic leaders to address some of growth's thornier issues head on and to provide the leadership that is so badly needed. . . .

Pragmatism as Innovation

Things change when tastes change. Health consciousness reached the point that McDonald's started putting salads on the menu. A little peer pressure helps. But we're driven not so much by ideology as by pragmatism.

The smart growth movement recognizes the futility of lecturing to the American people. Restrictions are passé [behind the times]. Nobody is drawing big maps anymore that have color-coded zones for where development can and can't go. Those are the maps that can just be put on a shelf when the next administration comes in. The smartest of the smart growth governments are concentrating on changing zoning, the DNA of growth, on steering funding toward infrastructure in built-up places, and on taking away the constraints that hobble good growth. Consumers have to take it from there.

Recently the movement's top leaders have been paying consultants to walk them through a process called "framing," which seeks to connect with a broader audience on shared values. When thinking about growth, the consultants advise, some of the hot-button terms are personal liberty, responsibility to family, and safety. Conservation and preservation are also common values. There's a lot to work with there—as long as smart growth stays disciplined in its message, as the champion of more choice and freedom.

In the absence of a Surgeon General's warning on sprawl, connecting on values is a clever way to try to channel shifting consumer demands. Developers have a new paradigm all ready to go. It's a new system just waiting to be implemented, waiting to catch on in its own self-propagating process, like putting music on CDs and then iPods instead of records and cassettes. Consumers have the power to make sprawl the relic all those drafting-table revolutionaries so dearly want it to be.

Organizations to Contact

The editors have compiled the following list of organizations concerned with the issues debated in this book. The descriptions are derived from materials provided by the organizations. All have publications or information available for interested readers. The list was compiled on the date of publication of the present volume; the information provided here may change. Readers need to remember that many organizations take several weeks or longer to respond to inquiries.

Alliance to Save Energy

1850 M Street, NW, Suite 600, Washington, DC   20036
(202) 857-0666 • fax: (202) 331-9588
e-mail: info@ase.org
website: www.ase.org

Founded in 1977, the Alliance to Save Energy is a non-profit coalition of business, government, environmental and consumer leaders that supports energy efficiency as a cost-effective energy resource and advocates energy-efficiency policies. To carry out its mission, the Alliance to Save Energy undertakes research, educational programs, and policy advocacy, designs and implements energy-efficiency projects, promotes technology development and deployment, and builds public-private partnerships in the U.S. and other countries. In addition to a regular e-newsletter, the Alliance to Save Energy website features a number of research and position papers, including "Energy Efficiency Potential in American Buildings" and "Conservation Is Not a Four-Letter Word."

American Society of Heating, Refrigerating, and Air Conditioning Engineers (ASHRAE)

1791 Tullie Circle NE, Atlanta, GA   30329
(800) 527-4723 • fax: (404) 321-5478

e-mail: ashrae@ashrae.org
website: www.ashrae.org

Founded in 1894, ASHRAE is an international organization that works to advance heating, ventilation, air conditioning and refrigeration to serve humanity and promote a sustainable world through research, standards writing, publishing and continuing education. In addition to a national conference, ASHRAE regularly publishes position papers, *ASHRAE Journal, ASHRAE Insights*, and several newsletters. Some of the recent publications available on its website include "Climate Change" and "Building Sustainability."

Ecocity Builders

339 15th Street, Suite 208, Oakland, CA   94612
Phone/Fax: (510) 444-4508
website: http://www.ecocitybuilders.org/

Ecocity Builders is a nonprofit organization dedicated to reshaping cities for the long-term health of human and natural systems. The organization develops and implements policy, design, and educational tools to reverse patterns of sprawl and excessive consumption; works to shift policies to prioritize walking, bicycling, and transit to reduce dependence on automobiles; and strives to restore biodiversity in cities in the form of creeks, gardens, parks, farms, and greenways.

Energy Star Program

1200 Pennsylvania Ave NW, Washington, DC   20460
(888) 782-7937
website: www.energystar.gov

In 1992 the US Environmental Protection Agency (EPA) introduced energy star as a voluntary labeling program designed to identify and promote energy-efficient products to reduce greenhouse gas emissions. In 1996, EPA partnered with the US Department of Energy and the Energy Star label is now on major appliances, office equipment, lighting, home electronics, and more and covers new homes and commercial and industrial buildings. In addition to annual reports and regular podcasts, the Energy Star website offers a number of publications, including energy-saving advisory reports, guidelines for new homes, and checklists for home improvements.

Environmental News Network (ENN)
402 North B St., Fairfield, IA   52556
(641) 472-2790 • fax: (641) 472-2790
website: www.enn.com

Since 1993, ENN has been educating the world about environmental issues. Its website offers environmental news, live chats, daily feature stories, forums for debate, audio, video, and more in an effort to provide unbiased information about current environmental debates. Some recent ENN publications have focused on ocean pollution, Spain's sustainability policies, and the connection between automobile emissions and the demise of coral reefs.

Environmental Protection Agency (EPA)
U.S. EPA, 1200 Pennsylvania Avenue, NW,
Washington, DC   20460
(202) 272-0167
website: www.epa.gov

Since 1970, EPA has been working for cleaner, healthier water, land, and air to protect human health and the environment. EPA works to develop and enforce regulations that implement environmental laws enacted by Congress. In addition to maintaining a database of environmental-related hotlines and clearinghouses, EPA offers a number of online publications, including "Air Quality and Emissions Trends Report" and *Healthy Buildings, Healthy People: A Vision for the 21st Century*.

International Centre for Sustainable Cities
205-1525 West 8th Avenue, Vancouver,
British Columbia V6J 1T5 Canada
(604) 569-0965 • fax: (604) 569-0975
website: http://sustainablecities.net/

Sustainable Cities was founded in Canada in 1993 as a partnership between government, the private sector and civil society organizations. The organization works to bring the idea of urban sustainability into practical action. Sustainable Cities has a core staff based in Vancouver, and an international panel of advisors, partner organizations, and associates in other cities.

Smart Growth America (SGA)

1707 L St NW, Suite 1050, Washington, DC   20036
(202) 207-3355 • fax: (202) 207-3349
e-mail: sga@smartgrowthamerica.org
website: http://smartgrowthamerica.org

SGA is a coalition of national, state and local organizations working to improve the ways that cities and towns are planned. The coalition includes many national organizations advocating on behalf of historic preservation, the environment, farmland and open space preservation, and neighborhood revitalization. The SGA website offers a number of resources, including such publications as "Growing Cooler: The Evidence on Urban Development and Climate Change" and "Vacant Properties: The True Cost to Communities."

Sustainable Buildings Industry Council (SBIC)

1112 16th St., NW, Ste. 240, Washington, DC   20036
(202) 628-7400 • fax: (202) 393-5043
e-mail: SBIC@SBICouncil.org
website: www.sbicouncil.org

Since 1980, SBIC has been a council of building associations committed to high-performance design and construction in conjunction with the fields of architecture, engineering, building systems and materials, product manufacturing, energy analysis, and "whole building" design. In addition to provide online tools for building industry professionals, SBIC also publishes reports about sustainable building practices. Some of SBIC's recent publications include *Green Building Guidelines: Meeting the Demand for Low-Energy, Resource-Efficient Homes* and *High-Performance School Buildings Resource and Strategy Guide*.

United Nations Division for Sustainable Development (UNDSD)

Two United Nations Plaza, Room DC2-2220,
New York, NY   10017 USA
(212) 963-8102 • fax: (212) 963-4260
website: www.un.org/esa/sustdev/

The UN Division for Sustainable Development provides leadership and is an authoritative source of expertise within the United Nations system on sustainable development. The UNDSD maintains a database of world statistics on sustainability and a collection of news reports on current sustainable activities around the world. In addition to position statements and FAQ sheets, the UNDSD website offers a number of other publications, including *Trends in Sustainable Development and Sustainable Consumption* and *Production: Promoting Climate-Friendly Household Consumption Patterns.*

U.S. Green Building Council (USGBC)

2101 L Street NW, Ste. 500, Washington, DC   20037
(202) 828-7422 • fax: (202) 828-5110
e-mail: info@usgbc.org
website: www.usgbc.org

USGBC is a non-profit association composed of more than 12,000 organizations from across the building industry that are working to advance structures that are environmentally responsible, profitable, and healthy places to live and work. USGBC's major effort is LEED (Leadership in Energy and Environmental Design), a voluntary, consensus-based national rating system for developing high-performance, sustainable buildings. USGBC offers online courses and other educational materials, including a number of publications, such as *GreenSource* and "A National Green Building Research Agenda."

Bibliography

Books

Timothy Beatley *Green Urbanism: Learning from European Cities.* Washington, DC: Island, 2000.

Eugenie L. Birch and Susan M. Wachter *Growing Greener Cities: Urban Sustainability in the Twenty-First Century.* Philadelphia, PA: University of Pennsylvania, 2008.

Ellen Dunham-Jones and June Williamson *Retrofitting Suburbia: Urban Design Solutions for Redesigning Suburbs.* Hoboken, NJ: Wiley & Sons, 2009.

Douglas Farr *Sustainable Urbanism: Urban Design with Nature.* Hoboken, NJ: Wiley & Sons, 2008.

Joan Fitzgerald *Emerald Cities: Urban Sustainability and Economic Development.* New York: Oxford University, 2010.

David Gordon, editor *Green Cities: Ecologically Sound Approaches to Urban Space.* Montreal (Canada): Black Rose Books, 1996.

Mathew E. Kahn *Green Cities: Urban Growth and the Environment.* Washington, DC: Brookings Institute, 2006.

Stephen Lehmann *The Principals of Green Urbanism: Regenerating the Post-Industrial City.* London: Earthscan, 2010.

David Owen — *Green Metropolis: Why Living Smaller, Living Closer, and Driving Less Are Keys to Sustainability.* New York: Riverhead, 2009.

Douglas R. Porter — *Making Smart Growth Work.* Washington, DC: Urban Land Institute, 2002.

Kent E. Portney — *Taking Sustainable Cities Seriously: Economic Development, the Environment, and Quality of Life in American Cities.* Cambridge, MA: MIT, 2003.

Richard Register — *EcoCities: Rebuilding Cities in Balance with Nature.* Gabriola Island, BC (Canada): New Society, 2006.

Mary Sonderstorm — *Green City: People, Nature, & Urban Life.* Montreal (Canada): Vehicule, 2006.

Zhenghong Tang — *Eco-City and Green Community: The Evolution of Planning Theory and Practice.* Hauppauge, NY: Nova Science, 2010.

Jerry Yudelson — *Green Building Through Integrated Design.* Columbus, OH: McGraw-Hill, 2008.

Periodicals

Linda Baker — "Green at City Scale," *Governing*, August 2009.

Tom Bradford | "Cohousing & Ecovillage Development," *Synthesis/Regeneration*, Fall 2009.

Nathan Cherry and Kurt Nagle | "Essential Element of Sustainable Design," *Planning*, March 2010.

Kathy Finn | "It's a Better Day in the Neighborhood," *New Orleans Magazine*, March 2010.

Will Galloway | "Of Suburbs and Cities," *Town and Country Planning*, July–August 2009.

Leah Harnack | "Sustainable Maintenance," *Mass Transit*, July–August 2009.

Justin Harrington | "Time to Change Our Habits," *Mississippi Business Journal*, March 30, 2009.

Moria Herbst | "Eco-Cites: Building a Comeback?" *Business Week Online*, September 1, 2009.

Benjamin A. Herman | "Embracing Sustainability in Community Plans," *Planning*, April 2010.

Karrie Jacobs | "Urban Utopias," *Travel & Leisure*, January 2010.

Will La Page | "Parks Are How We Write Our Poetry on the Land," *Parks & Recreation*, August 2009.

Diana Lind | "Electric Cars Are Still Cars," *Earth Island Journal*, Summer 2010.

Adal Mirza "A Model of Sustainability," *Middle East Economic Digest*, April 3, 2009.

Edmund O'Sullivan "Abu Dhabi Sets the Standard," *Middle East Economic Digest*, October 2009.

Janet Oswald "Planning for Urban Agriculture," *Plan Canada*, Summer 2009.

Stephen Peck "Green Jobs and Training," *Landscape & Irrigation*, April 2010.

Suzanne Rynne "Green Community Planning in the U.S.A.," *Town and County Planning*, March 2009.

Pamela Ann Smith "Jeddah: Planning a World-Class City," *Middle East*, November 2009.

Chris Turner "The Ideal Urban Form," *Plan Canada*, Winter 2009.

John Woods "Going Green: More than Jumping on Bandwagon," *Mississippi Business Journal*, March 30, 2009.

Index